Cambridge Elements ☰

Elements in Philosophy of Law
edited by
George Pavlakos
University of Glasgow
Gerald J. Postema
University of North Carolina at Chapel Hill
Kenneth M. Ehrenberg
University of Surrey
Sally Zhu
University of Sheffield

THE NATURE OF AUTHORITY

Kenneth Einar Himma
University of Zagreb

CAMBRIDGE
UNIVERSITY PRESS

CAMBRIDGE
UNIVERSITY PRESS

Shaftesbury Road, Cambridge CB2 8EA, United Kingdom

One Liberty Plaza, 20th Floor, New York, NY 10006, USA

477 Williamstown Road, Port Melbourne, VIC 3207, Australia

314–321, 3rd Floor, Plot 3, Splendor Forum, Jasola District Centre,
New Delhi – 110025, India

103 Penang Road, #05–06/07, Visioncrest Commercial, Singapore 238467

Cambridge University Press is part of Cambridge University Press & Assessment,
a department of the University of Cambridge.

We share the University's mission to contribute to society through the pursuit of
education, learning and research at the highest international levels of excellence.

www.cambridge.org
Information on this title: www.cambridge.org/9781009507813

DOI: 10.1017/9781009255790

First published 2024

A catalogue record for this publication is available from the British Library

ISBN 978-1-009-50781-3 Hardback
ISBN 978-1-009-25581-3 Paperback
ISSN 2631-5815 (online)
ISSN 2631-5807 (print)

The Nature of Authority

Elements in Philosophy of Law

DOI: 10.1017/9781009255790
First published online: December 2024

Kenneth Einar Himma
University of Zagreb

Author for correspondence: Kenneth Einar Himma, khimma@gmail.com

Abstract: *The Nature of Authority* provides a comprehensive theory of the nature of authoritative guidance. It argues that the following claims exhaust the constitutive properties of authoritative tellings: authoritative tellings (1) tell subjects what to do; (2) give rise to reasons to comply; (3) are issued by personal beings and govern the behavior of personal beings; (4) are issued by rationally competent beings and govern the behavior of rationally competent beings; (5) are issued under a claim of right that counts as plausible in virtue of being grounded in a system to which subjects acquiesce as governing their behavior; (6) are issued by beings with the power to impose their will on subjects with respect to what they do; (7) create obligations to comply; and (8) are backed by a threat of detriment that is reasonably contrived to deter enough noncompliance to enable the system to minimally achieve its ends. Claim (8) can be inferred from each of the above claims except for claim (3).

Keywords: practical authority, epistemic authority, law, jurisprudence, conceptual analysis

ISBNs: 9781009507813 (HB), 9781009255813 (PB), 9781009255790 (OC)
ISSNs: 2631-5815 (online), 2631-5807 (print)

Contents

Contents

All writing is pigshit.

—Antonin Artaud

Preface

The concept of practical authority plays an indispensable role in theorizing about the nature of law. Law might not be the most paradigmatic species of practical authority; however, it is indisputable that law is a locus of such authority and that mandatory legal prescriptions, norms, and directives count as authoritative because they count as law:[1] it is uncontentious, bordering on banal, that courts have something that counts as legal authority over persons appearing before them and that court orders count as legally authoritative.

Despite its centrality to our jurisprudential theorizing and practices, no one has tried to formulate a comprehensive conceptual theory of practical authority. The most influential theory of practical authority, Raz's service conception, does not so much as purport to fully articulate its nature. This should not be thought a defect of the service conception because it is equally, if not more, concerned with the following normative issues: (i) the conditions under which authority is morally justified, (ii) the standards governing how subjects should reason with authoritative tellings, and (iii) the normative considerations that authoritative tellings should be based on.

The reason we lack a comprehensive conceptual theory of practical authority is that the issues associated with its moral and practical justification are regarded as being of more social importance – and rightly so. It matters a great deal, for instance, whether the practices associated with legal authority are morally justified. It is not surprising, then, that theorists would devote more energy to the normative moral issues than to the descriptive conceptual issues.

Even so, these conceptual issues have been strangely disparaged as "uninteresting"[2] and not worth working on. It should be clear that we cannot work out a theory of legitimate authority (i.e., what it should be, as a matter of political morality) without understanding its nature (i.e., what it is, as a conceptual matter).[3] For instance, the moral issues regarding the justification of

---

[1] Hereinafter I will refer to mandatory prescriptions, general and particular, that have their source in some personal being as *tellings* because they tell people what to do.

[2] Sigh. As if these folks have epistemically privileged access to some God's-eye notion of what's interesting that the rest of us lack.

[3] But this is not why I work on conceptual issues. I find conceptual and metaphysical issues, including those characterized as *metaethical*, more challenging than theoretical or applied normative issues because they are more abstract. And I can't help thinking that some of the hostility directed at conceptual jurisprudence has to do with its difficulty. It is quite telling that philosophers in other areas never whine about conceptual analysis, metaphysics, or metaethics.

practical authority obviously depend on whether it is inherently coercive; the most morally salient feature of legal authority, after all, is that it is frequently exercised to incarcerate people. Without a theory of the concept, it is impossible to develop a general theory of moral legitimacy that enables us to evaluate our systems of authoritative guidance in a systematic, rather than piecemeal, way.

The Nature of Authority attempts to rectify this omission, arguing for two main theses. The first thesis is that the indented claim below exhausts the constitutive properties of authoritative tellings in the sense that any claim truly describing a constitutive property of authoritative tellings that does not appear among the properties listed in this claim can be derived from claims that do:

> Authoritative tellings (1) tell subjects what to do; (2) give rise to reasons to comply; (3) are issued by personal beings and govern the behavior of personal beings; (4) are issued by rational beings and govern the behavior of rational beings; (5) are issued under a claim of right that counts as plausible in virtue of being grounded in a system that subjects accept, or acquiesce to, as governing their acts; (6) are issued by beings with the power to impose their will on subjects with respect to what they do; and (7) create obligations to comply.

The second main thesis is that only tellings backed by the threat of a sanction count as authoritative (the Sanctions Thesis). This Element argues that the Sanctions Thesis can justifiably be inferred from all but one of the above claims, either as a logical implication of those claims or as the best explanation of why they are true, the exception being claim (3) that authoritative tellings are issued by personal beings and govern the behavior of such beings. All but one of these properties, I conclude, are uniquely explained by the Sanctions Thesis.

It is crucial to note at the outset that the analysis of this Element is nonpartisan in the sense that it does not assume any conceptual claims about law beyond the truism that law is, by nature, a social artifact. It is *conceptually* possible for the norms of morality to exist in a world without intelligent beings, as would be true if morality is objective rather than conventional in nature. Morality would simply lack application in that world. But it is not conceptually possible for a system of law to exist in a world without intelligent beings. Since no remotely plausible natural law theory denies that law counts as an artifact in virtue of being brought into existence by our social practices, this truism is compatible with positivism and every plausible antipositivist theory. Since law is a species of authoritative guidance, this is as it should be.

PART I   PRELIMINARY CONSIDERATIONS

1 Introduction

This Element articulates a theory of the nature of practical authority, but what does it mean to speak of the "nature" of something? The nature of a kind K is exhausted by the properties something must have to count as an instance of K – that is, its existence conditions.[4] Otherwise put, the nature of K is exhausted by the properties that *constitute* anything that instantiates them as a K – its *constitutive properties*, as I hereinafter describe them.

Consider the concept of a bachelor. *Merriam-Webster* defines the term *bachelor* as "an unmarried man."[5] If the Pope does not count as a bachelor, as some believe, because he is ineligible for marriage, then this definition does not exhaust the constitutive properties of bachelorhood; in this case, it is also a necessary condition for an unmarried man to count as a bachelor that he is eligible for marriage. But if the Pope counts as a bachelor and there are no other plausible counterexamples, this definition exhausts the constitutive properties of bachelorhood. Accordingly, if either conditional exhausts the constitutive properties of bachelorhood, that conditional fully explicates its nature.

A theory of the nature of K is best understood as an empirically grounded theory of *our* concept of K. Since, as discussed below, the only concepts to which we have epistemic access are defined by what we do with words, a theory of the nature of K is best understood as an empirically grounded theory of *our* conceptual practices for using the corresponding concept-term *K*: a theory of the nature of bachelorhood, then, is an empirically grounded theory of our conceptual practices for using *bachelor*; a theory of the nature of authority is an empirically grounded theory of our conceptual practices for using *authority*; a theory of the nature of law is an empirically grounded theory of our conceptual practices for using *law*; and so on.

The content of *our* conceptual practices for using any term is fixed by two types of consideration: (a) our conventions for using it, which are compiled by lexicographers and roughly summarized in dictionary definitions; and (b) shared philosophical assumptions, if any, about the nature of the associated kind that condition the application of these semantic conventions in hard cases.

There is thus a division of labor between lexicography and philosophy in addressing conceptual matters. Lexicography is concerned just to report the content of our conventions for using a word; these conventions are *roughly*

---

[4]   General terms – like *law, water, blue, proposition* – define kinds (of thing). Our concepts pick out kinds.

[5]   www.merriam-webster.com/dictionary/bachelor.

summarized by dictionary definitions and, for this reason, tend to be over-inclusive or underinclusive in determining the reference class of the term of interest. Philosophy, in contrast, is concerned to articulate a more complete, and thus more accurate, account of a kind's constitutive properties by explicating the shared assumptions about its nature that qualify the application of those conventions in hard cases.

That a dictionary definition is vulnerable to counterexamples – as is true if the Pope does not count as a bachelor – is not necessarily a defect. Dictionary definitions are reports of a word's meaning that are intended merely to provide enough information about how to use it to constitute a speaker as *competent* using it. But one can be competent using a word without knowing how it applies in hard cases, if any. One does not need to know whether, for instance, the Pope counts as a bachelor to be competent using the term *bachelor*.

Competence with a word is, after all, a baseline capacity that is wholly constituted by an ability to apply it in easy cases. One counts as competent using a word if one can use it in the vast majority of circumstances one is likely to encounter. If you know, for instance, that *law* is, as *Cambridge Dictionary* defines it, "a rule, usually made by a government, that is used to order the way in which a society behaves,"[6] then you are competent with the word – even if you don't have a clue whether there can be a system without sanctions that counts as one of law. Just knowing this definition is enough to enable you to ascertain, at least roughly, which norms count as law in any country you might be visiting.

There are two methodological approaches to analyzing the nature of a kind. Modest conceptual analysis is concerned to explicate the nature of a kind as it is wholly determined by what we do with language – that is, it is concerned to explicate *our* conceptual practices with respect to some term of interest.[7] Immodest conceptual analysis, though it purports to analyze concepts that are in some mysterious sense *ours*, is concerned to explicate the nature of a kind as determined independently of what we do with language.

This Element adopts modest conceptual analysis for two reasons. First, I don't have a clue how to ascertain the nature of a kind if it is determined independently of what we do with language – and, to be candid, neither do you. Second, I believe that we can learn something important about ourselves by understanding how we use language to organize the world of our experience. We adopt a language to talk about features of the world that we find salient. Understanding the underlying conceptual practices can thus teach us something

---

[6]　https://dictionary.cambridge.org/dictionary/english/law.

[7]　For a defense of modest conceptual analysis, see Frank Jackson, *From Metaphysics to Ethics: A Defense of Conceptual Analysis* (Oxford University Press, 2000).

worthwhile about not only what we value but also how we conceive ourselves and society.

On either approach, conceptual analysis is descriptive in virtue of being concerned to explicate what the content of the concept of interest *is* (what the term means), as opposed to what it *ought to be* (what the term should mean). For what it is worth, I am skeptical of the idea that we can improve our world simply by changing our conceptual practices in any other ways than to make them more rigorous or to remove words used for the sole purpose of hurting other people. Either way, ascertaining whether these practices should be changed is the province of conceptual engineering. Conceptual engineering and conceptual analysis are hence different, but complementary, projects.

At the outset, I should explain one feature of the methodology that is likely to strike readers as nonstandard – namely, that I frequently rely on dictionary definitions. But I cite definitions only to justify claims that are aptly described as "truisms" about a term in virtue of being transparently entailed by our semantic conventions for using it. Although the vast majority of these claims strike my mind as uncontentious, they would otherwise have to be assumed without defense. While it is common for philosophers to claim some proposition is a truism without giving a defense, this often leads to futile disputes about intuitions that I prefer to avoid.

The point of relying on dictionary definitions to even this limited extent is to defend what I take to be conceptual truisms that would otherwise have to go without defense. If a proposition is transparently entailed by *our* conventions for using a term and you disagree it expresses a truism, then, absent exceptional circumstances, you are confused about the term's meaning. My use of definitions is intended simply to preempt disagreements about whether some claim expresses a conceptual truism. While this should be clear from the discussion, I feel obliged to explain that these definitions do no heavy lifting whatsoever, because, as I have discovered to my profound puzzlement, philosophers are suspicious of dictionaries.

To dispel these bizarre suspicions, it is helpful to note that lexicographers – unlike philosophers – are required to get training in the methods of the social sciences in the course of their professional education. Lexicographers, unlike philosophers, are social scientists. It is utterly crucial to understand both that our conventions for using a word are empirically determined and that the content of those conventions can be reliably discerned only through the empirical methods of the social sciences. Although one must be competent with a word to ascertain the deeper assumptions about the nature of the associated kind, the canons of ordinary usage cannot simply be intuited from the privilege of the philosophical armchair. They must be learned empirically.

None of this assumes dictionary definitions are infallible. These definitions can be mistaken in hard cases, but that is because our conventions do not even purport to address those cases. They can also be mistaken when our conventions are being worked out for a new word or are in the process of being revised; such revisions can occur when an existing word is considered harmful or when science has revealed something new about a kind we thought we had a handle on.[8] While a dictionary definition can be inaccurate, the mistakes are generally confined to hard cases because the polling techniques deployed to ascertain our conventions are scientifically sound. Absent exceptional circumstances, a dictionary definition will not be systematically mistaken for this reason.

One last observation would be helpful. I do not claim that a comprehensive theory of the nature of practical authority can be derived from just the definitions of the relevant terms. The point of citing definitions is to minimize the number of potentially contestable claims that must be assumed. My analysis sometimes relies on claims that I assume without defense because they seem uncontentious. But this is simply unavoidable. Every argument has to be grounded in claims that are assumed; trying to defend every claim in an argument would lead to an infinite regress. For this reason, the most I (or anyone else, for that matter) can do is minimize the number of assumptions in the argument. That is one of the helpful things that my reliance on dictionary definitions enables me to do.

2 Metaphysics, Modality, and Conceptual Analysis

Conceptual analysis is concerned to explicate the nature of the kind referred to by the term of interest, but the nature of a kind is determined by the properties that constitute something as an instance of that kind – that is, the properties something must have to count as an instance of that kind: the nature of a bachelor is determined by the properties constituting something as a bachelor; the nature of authority is determined by the properties constituting something as an authority; the nature of law is determined by the properties constituting something as a law; and so on.

Constitution differs from causation in the following respect. Being unmarried might have many causal effects – such as loneliness. But being unmarried does not *cause* a man to be a bachelor. Whatever it is that causally explains why he is unmarried causally explains why he is a bachelor. If he is unmarried because he is an asshole, then it is the fact he is an asshole that causally explains why he is unmarried *and* hence why he is a bachelor. But being an asshole is not what

---

[8] This appears to be the case with the term *water*. See n. 10 for a discussion of the claim that water is H_2O and its implications with respect to whether it is in the nature of H_2O that it is water.

constitutes him as a bachelor. What constitutes him as a bachelor is that he is unmarried, because someone counts as a bachelor in virtue of being an unmarried man.

Claims about the nature of a kind are necessarily true, if true at all: to say it is part of the nature of a bachelor that bachelors are unmarried is to say it is necessarily true that bachelors are unmarried; to say it is part of the nature of authority that it tells people what to do is to say it is necessarily true that authorities tell people what to do; to say it is part of the nature of a legal system that it consists of norms is to say it is necessarily true that a legal system consists of norms; and so on.

There are three kinds of *descriptively* necessary statements, which differ according to what explains why the instances of that kind are necessarily true.[9] To begin, a descriptive statement is *logically necessary* just in case it is deducible from some set of favored logical axioms. What explains why a descriptive statement is *logically* necessary is therefore that it can be validly deduced from the favored axioms, which are assumed by the system to be logically necessary.

It is important to note that the axioms of a system of logic define the behavior of its connectives, quantifiers, and any other operators it contains. Standard propositional logics, for instance, include the "law of contraposition" as an axiom. This expresses the truism that, for all sentences p and q, $[(p \rightarrow q) \rightarrow (\sim q \rightarrow \sim p)]$. Similarly, standard modal logics include the schema that, for all sentences p, $(\Box p \rightarrow p)$ as an axiom. This expresses the truism that, for any sentence p, if p is necessarily true, p is true. Logical necessity is determined by the *form* of a sentence – and not its content – as that form is constructed by the arrangement of its connectives, quantifiers, and operators.

Metaphysical and nomological necessity, in contrast, are determined by the content of a sentence. The claim, for instance, that no squares are round is metaphysically necessary because it cannot be deduced from just the favored logical axioms defining the behavior of the relevant connectives and quantifiers; nor can it be deduced from those axioms with the help of statements that describe causal regularities in the universe. Its necessity depends on the content of the concepts of square and round.

A claim is hence metaphysically necessary just in case it follows from the union of some set of favored logical axioms and some set of favored metaphysical claims – that is, claims that are true no matter what laws correctly describe causal

---

[9] Moral claims are thought to be normatively necessary, if true. Most moral theorists believe such claims are true in virtue of their content, but some – so-called divine command theorists – believe they are true in virtue of being commanded by a perfect deity. True moral norms would count as authoritative tellings on the latter, but not the former, view.

regularities in this world but that do not follow from just the favored axioms. Inasmuch as the favored metaphysical claims are true in virtue of their content, so is any claim that is validly deduced from them. Accordingly, the truth of a metaphysically necessary claim cannot be explained in terms of just the favored axioms and claims describing causal regularities in the material world.

There are two species of metaphysical necessity: conceptual and nonconceptual. A metaphysically necessary truth counts as *conceptual* if and only if it is true in virtue of how we use the constituent words: the claim all bachelors are unmarried is conceptual because it is true just in virtue of the way that we use the term *bachelor*. A metaphysically necessary truth counts as *nonconceptual*, in contrast, if it is true but not just in virtue of how we use the constituent words. The claim that nothing can be red and green all over is nonconceptual because it is true no matter what the laws of nature happen to be but does not follow from just the union of the set of favored logical axioms and a set of claims that fully describe how we use the word – that is, our conceptual practices.

A claim is nomologically necessary just in case it follows from the union of some set of favored logical axioms, some set of favored metaphysical claims, and a set of claims that correctly describe *necessary* causal regularities in our world (such as those of physics) but does not follow from the union of the favored logical axioms and favored metaphysical claims. The claim that water freezes at 32°F counts as nomologically necessary in virtue of being deducible *only* from a set that includes claims we believe correctly describe these causal regularities.[10]

Claims about the nature of a kind count as metaphysical since they are necessarily true, if true, *and* cannot be deduced from any set consisting of just favored logical axioms and claims describing causal regularities in our world. It is clear that claims about the nature of a kind cannot be deduced from an axiom schema like $[p \rightarrow (q \rightarrow p)]$. It is likewise clear that claims about the nature of a kind cannot be deduced from nomological claims like $e=mc^2$. Claims about the nature of a kind are metaphysical, then, because true claims about the nature of a kind are necessary but cannot be deduced from any set consisting of just logical axioms and claims correctly describing causal regularities. Claims describing the constitutive properties of a kind – that is, those properties constituting something as a member of that kind – also count as metaphysical because those properties define its nature.

---

[10] The character of the claim that water is necessarily composed of H_2O molecules is not clear. If our semantic conventions for using the term preclude characterizing anything as *water* that is not composed of H_2O, then it is conceptually and metaphysically necessary. If they do not preclude characterizing entities not composed of H_2O molecules as *water*, then it is nomologically necessary.

Whether or not the truth-value of some claim about the nature of a kind can change depends on which methodology is adopted. Modest conceptual analysis attempts to identify true claims about the nature of a kind that are wholly conditioned by our conceptual practices and hence assumes that the truth-value of claims about the nature of a kind is determined by our conceptual practices. If these practices change in salient particulars, then so will the truth-value of any related claims about the nature of the associated kind. Immodest conceptual analysis attempts to identify true claims about a kind's nature that are *not* wholly conditioned by our conceptual practices and hence assumes that the truth-value of claims describing the nature of a kind is determined utterly independently of those practices. If the truth-value of a claim describing some kind's nature changes, it is not, according to immodest conceptual analysis, because our conceptual practices have changed. True claims describing the nature of a kind are *conditionally necessary* on modest conceptual analysis but not on immodest conceptual analysis.

It is worth noting one salient difference between the locution *constitutive properties* and another phrase sometimes used to describe the properties defining the nature of a kind. Unlike the locution *essential properties*, the phrase *constitutive properties* neither implies nor insinuates that the nature of a kind cannot change and thus does not imply a problematic conceptual "essentialism." Given that immodest conceptual analysis assumes that the nature of a kind cannot change, the properties constituting that nature are aptly characterized as *essential properties* in this stronger sense.

3 Two Kinds of Authority: Epistemic and Practical

Our conceptual practices distinguish two kinds of authority. Epistemic authority prescribes what ought to be *believed* through assertions that create reasons to believe those assertions: an oncologist's assertion that a patient has cancer gives rise to a reason to believe she has cancer; an attorney's assertion that a client should settle a lawsuit gives rise to a reason to believe she should settle it; and so on. Practical authority prescribes what should be *done* through utterances that give rise to reasons to do what those utterances say should be done: a sergeant telling a soldier under her command to march gives rise to a reason to march; a judge telling a witness to answer a question gives rise to a reason to answer it; and so on.[11]

---

[11] As *Cambridge* explains the distinction, the term *authority* means "[t]he power or right to give orders . . . and enforce obedience" and "the power to control or demand obedience from others" and "the ability to influence other people . . . because you . . . have a lot of knowledge." https://dictionary.cambridge.org/us/dictionary/english/authority. The first definition is concerned with practical authority and, it is worth noting, supports the Sanctions Thesis, whereas the second is concerned with epistemic authority.

Epistemic and practical authority are logically independent because each species of authority has at least one constitutive property that the other one lacks: *P* counts as having *epistemic* authority on whether *Q* should perform certain acts *only if P*'s views on whether *Q* should perform them are more likely to be correct than *Q*'s because *P* has expertise on whether *Q* should perform them.[12] In contrast, whether *P* has *practical* authority to direct *Q* to perform them does not depend at all on whether *P* has expertise constituting *P* as an epistemic authority on whether *Q* should perform them.[13] Though someone with practical authority might have such expertise, it is not a necessary condition for *P* to count as having practical authority to tell *Q* to perform certain acts that she also counts as having epistemic authority on whether *Q* should perform them.

Conversely, it is not a necessary condition for *P* to count as an epistemic authority on whether *Q* should perform such acts that *P* counts as having practical authority to direct *Q* to perform them. Whether *P* counts as having practical authority to tell *Q* to do s depends on whether *P* is minimally efficacious in inducing *Q* to do s.[14] However, whether *P* counts as having epistemic authority on whether *Q* should do s does not depend on whether *P* is minimally efficacious in inducing *Q* to do s. No matter how many patients die because they do not follow an oncologist's recommendations, the oncologist counts as having epistemic authority pertaining to the treatment of cancer provided that she has the requisite expertise. The claim that *P* counts as having practical authority over *Q* is hence logically independent of the claim that *P* counts as having epistemic authority over *Q*.

4 The Razian Theory of Practical Authority

There has been a great deal of philosophical effort devoted to identifying the principles that a system of authoritative guidance must meet to count as morally or practically justified,[15] but comparatively little philosophical effort has been

---

[12] I say "only if," instead of "if and only if," because the fact that *P* knows more than *Q* about some topic does not suffice to constitute *P* as having epistemic authority on that topic because it does not suffice to constitute *P* as having the conceptually requisite expertise on it.

[13] Raz believes that whether *P* has *legitimate* practical authority over *Q* depends on whether *P* has epistemic authority on what *Q* should do given the reasons that antecedently apply to *Q*. But whether some instance of authority is legitimate is a normative moral issue different from the descriptive conceptual issue of whether someone counts as having practical authority. Indeed, it is crucial to understand in this connection that Raz's distinction between merely de facto authority and authority per se acknowledges the banality that there can be morally illegitimate authority. He is absolutely clear, though this is often overlooked, that the latter refers only to legitimate authority.

[14] See Section 6 for more discussion of this efficacy condition.

[15] See, e.g., Harry Beran, *The Consent Theory of Political Obligation* (Croon Helm, 1987); Allen Buchanan, *Justice, Legitimacy and Self-Determination* (Oxford University Press, 2004);

expended on the conceptual issues of what constitutes a telling as authoritative and what constitutes someone as having practical authority.

Joseph Raz has had more to say about the nature of practical authority than anyone, but his theory of practical authority is as much concerned with normative issues, like how authority ought to be exercised and how subjects ought to reason with authoritative tellings, as with purely descriptive issues regarding the constitutive properties of practical authority. This section explicates his service conception of practical authority.

4.1 The Service Conception of Authority

Raz's service conception of authority consists of three theses: the Preemption, Dependence, and Normal Justification Theses. According to the Preemption Thesis, "[t]he fact that an authority requires performance of an action is a reason for its performance which is not to be added to all other relevant reasons when assessing what to do, but should replace some of them."[16] The Preemption Thesis therefore expresses two claims: (i) authoritative tellings give rise to reasons to comply as a matter of conceptual necessity; and (ii) subjects should treat them as *replacing* some of the reasons that would otherwise be applicable in their decision-making about what to do.[17]

Only claim (i) is conceptual. It asserts that every telling that counts as authoritative gives rise to a reason to comply, as a descriptive matter of fact. Claim (ii), in contrast, is a normative claim pertaining to how subjects should treat these reasons in their deliberations; it is therefore, in essence, a claim about what is required by the content of objective norms of practical reasoning – or, more accurately, a claim about what we (or perhaps people with the appropriate expertise) believe is required by these putatively objective standards.[18]

The Dependence Thesis is, by its own terms, a normative claim purporting to identify the reasons on which authoritative tellings should be based – namely,

---

David Estlund, *Democratic Authority* (Cambridge University Press, 2007); Leslie Green, *The Authority of the State* (Oxford University Press, 1989); John Locke, *Second Treatise on Civil Government*, ed. C. B MacPherson (Hackett, 1990); Robert Nozick, *Anarchy, State, and Utopia* (Basic Books, 1977); Plato, *Euthyphro, Apology and Crito*, trans. F. J. Church (Macmillan, 1948); John Rawls, *Political Liberalism* (Columbia University Press, 1996); Robert Paul Wolff, *In Defense of Anarchism* (Harper & Row, 1970). It bears repeating here that one cannot expect to reliably identify the relevant norms of morally legitimate authority without understanding what authority is by nature. If the project of descriptive conceptual analysis needs justification (sigh, it doesn't), that is more than enough to do the job.

[16] Joseph Raz, *Ethics in the Public Domain* (Clarendon Press, 1994), 214.   [17] Ibid.

[18] I put the matter this way because I do not think we have epistemic access to truths – whether conceptual, moral, or metaphysical – that are objective in the sense their truth values are determined entirely by mind-independent considerations. But nothing turns on my putting it this way.

those that "apply to the subjects of those directives and [that] bear on the circumstances covered by the directives."[19] The Dependence Thesis, as is true of claim (ii) of the Preemption Thesis, purports to be an objective requirement of practical reasoning that applies to the decisions of those with practical authority. Although Raz believes that the Dependence Thesis is necessarily true, its necessity is not determined by our conceptual practices; it is determined instead, on his view, by the content of the relevant norms of practical reasoning.

The Normal Justification Thesis is, by its own terms, a claim describing what justifies practical authority. As Raz articulates it:

> The normal and primary way to establish that a person should be acknow-ledged to have authority over another person involves showing that the alleged subject is likely better to comply with reasons which apply to him (other than the alleged authoritative directives) if he accepts the directives of the alleged authority as authoritatively binding, and tries to follow them, than if he tries to follow the reasons which apply to him directly.[20]

Given the language in which it is expressed, the Normal Justification Thesis can be interpreted as descriptive – though this is clearly not the interpretation Raz intends. The problem is that its language suggests that the Normal Justification Thesis is an empirical claim: thus construed, the Normal Justification Thesis is a claim about how authority is *normally* justified. But claims about how people "normally" do things are sociological, empirically descriptive, and contingent in character.[21] It should be clear both that Raz does not intend to make a sociological claim here and that he would not do so without attempting to provide the needed empirical evidence.[22]

4.2 Authoritative Tellings and Exclusionary Reasons

According to Raz's Exclusionary Thesis, any telling that counts as authoritative gives rise to a second-order exclusionary reason that bars the agent from *acting* on the reasons it is supposed to replace. An authoritative telling is thus doubly normative, according to the Exclusionary Thesis, in the following respect: it gives rise not only to a first-order reason to comply but also to a second-order

---

[19] Raz, *Ethics in the Public Domain*, 214.   [20] Ibid.

[21] There are a number of ways to construe the Normal Justification Thesis if it is normative. First, one can construe it as describing either the conditions in which *assertions* of authority are justified or the conditions in which *acceptance* of some authority's claim of right is justified. Second, one can construe it as a condition *sufficient* to justify authority or as a condition *necessary* to justify it. Finally, one can construe the Normal Justification Thesis either as an ontological claim about what constitutes authority as justified or as an epistemological claim about the most reliable way to ascertain whether a practical authority is justified – though the latter seems clearly false to me.

[22] But see Section 14 for an example of an instance in which Raz clearly makes an empirical claim without even attempting to provide the needed empirical evidence for it.

exclusionary reason that *protects* the first-order reason by barring a subject from acting on the excluded set of reasons.

While the Exclusionary Thesis may seem to be a claim about the nature of practical authority, it purports, in essence, to report what norms of practical reasoning require of us in deliberations about what we should do. It is thus a substantive normative claim about what norms of practical reasoning require – and not a descriptive conceptual claim about the constitutive properties of practical authority. As Raz acknowledges:

> The distinction between first-order and second-order reasons for action has not been recognized or discussed by philosophers. This is no doubt due at least in part to the fact that it is not reflected in any straightforward way in our use of the expressions of ordinary language. ... My claim is that a useful explication of the notions of strength, weight and overriding is possible but only at the cost of restricting their scope of application and that if we embark on such an explication the theory of conflict must allow for the existence of other logical types of conflicts and of conflict resolutions.[23]

Accordingly, Raz infers the claim there are objective exclusionary reasons from the content of what he believes are objective norms of practical reasoning because he rejects the idea, and correctly so, that the Exclusionary Thesis is true simply in virtue of how we use the relevant words. Rather, he believes that the Exclusionary Thesis is true because objective norms of practical rationality require subjects to consider the applicable exclusionary reasons when deliberating about whether to comply with an authoritative telling.

4.3 Practical Authority as the Power of Will-Imposition

There is one more piece to the Razian theory of practical authority, which he mentions only once and only in passing: an agent counts as having practical authority only if "effective in imposing [her] will on many over whom [she] claims authority."[24] It is clear this is a purely descriptive claim that purports to explicate a constitutive property of authoritative guidance and is, for that reason, a claim that purports to explicate its nature.

4.4 Conclusions

Raz's service conception is mixed in the sense it consists of both conceptual and normative elements. This, I think, is why Raz uses the term "conception" to

---

[23] Raz, *Practical Reason and Norms* (Oxford University Press, 1999), 36 (emphasis added). For more discussion of the Exclusionary Thesis, see Kenneth Einar Himma, "The Practical Otiosity of Exclusionary Reasons," *Canadian Journal of Jurisprudence* (forthcoming).

[24] Raz, *Ethics in the Public Domain*, 211.

describe his theory instead of the phrase "theory of the nature," which he uses to refer to his conceptual theory of *law*.[25] Though, in Section 5, I endorse his descriptive claims that authoritative guidance (i) gives rise to reasons to comply and (ii) is grounded in a power of will-imposition, this falls considerably short of a comprehensive theory of the nature of authoritative guidance. That is not, of course, to deny the social importance of his normative claims. But my concern in this Element is to defend purely descriptive claims about the nature of authoritative guidance. I am not in the least concerned here with moral legitimacy or justification.

PART II   THE EXISTENCE CONDITIONS OF PRACTICAL AUTHORITY

5 The Constitutive Properties of Authoritative Tellings

It is a conceptual truism that practical authority is exercised through the issuance of tellings that count as authoritative in virtue of satisfying the norms that confer such authority and constrain its scope. Whether a person P has practical authority over another person Q is determined by whether the relevant institutional, moral, or social norms confer a capacity on P to direct Q's behavior; this capacity is *norm-governed* in the sense that the relevant norms constrain the scope of practical authority by limiting what it is authorized to demand of its subjects. The existence conditions for both practical authority and authoritative guidance, then, are defined by the constitutive properties of authoritative tellings.

Part II of this Element argues that the following claim exhausts the constitutive properties of authoritative tellings in the sense that any claim correctly describing a constitutive property of authoritative tellings that does not appear among these properties listed in this claim can be derived from those that do: Authoritative tellings (1) tell subjects what to do; (2) create reasons to comply; (3) are issued by personal beings and govern the actions of personal beings; (4) are issued by rationally competent beings and govern the actions of rationally competent beings; (5) are issued under a claim of right that counts as plausible in virtue of being grounded in a system of norms that subjects at least acquiesce to; (6) are issued by beings with a power to impose their will on subjects with respect to what they do; and (7) create obligations to comply. Each of these claims strikes me as stating a conceptual truism about the nature of practical authority.[26]

---

[25] See, e.g., Joseph Raz, "About Morality and the Nature of Law," *American Journal of Jurisprudence*, vol. 48, no. 1 (2003), 1–15.

[26] The burden of persuasion falls on the critic to produce *plausible* counterexamples. This is nowhere near as easy as it may seem.

Part II attempts to show that only tellings backed by a sanction count as authoritative (the Sanctions Thesis); in particular, it argues the Sanctions Thesis can be inferred from each of claims (1) through (7), with the exception of (3)'s claim that authoritative tellings are issued by, and govern the behavior of, personal beings. It concludes that all but one of these constitutive properties are uniquely explained by the Sanctions Thesis.

It should be noted that the term *sanction*, for my purposes, has a broader application than is customary in legal philosophy. There is no requirement that detriment be punitive or as severe as the penalties of the criminal law to count as a sanction; even the threat of a failing grade satisfies the Sanctions Thesis to the extent it enables a teacher to evaluate her students' performance. It is enough, then, to constitute detriment as a sanction, for my ends, that it is reasonably likely, and therefore reasonably contrived, to minimally achieve the authority's ends – no matter how mild the detriment might be and regardless of whether it is intended to deter noncompliance.[27] If a slice of detriment is minimally equipped to do this job, then it counts for my purposes as a sanction.

6 Other Candidates for Constitutive Properties of Authoritative Tellings

There are, as far as I can tell, only three other presumptively plausible claims purporting to identify constitutive properties of authoritative tellings. But two of them are easily derived from claim (6) that practical authority is constituted, in part, by a power of will-imposition over what subjects do.

The first claim is that a telling counts as authoritative with respect to someone only if she accepts, or acquiesces to, the putative authority's claim of right over her. Two people must do something to stand in the authority relation as authority and subject: the teller must perform some verbal or nonverbal act that asserts the conceptually requisite claim of right over the subject in the course of telling her what she must do, and the subject must accept, or acquiesce to, the teller's claim of right over her by manifesting a disposition to comply when not initially inclined to do so.

---

[27] To count as an instance of an artifact kind, an artifact must be reasonably contrived to do what artifacts of that kind are standardly needed and used to do. To count as a car, for instance, a vehicle must be reasonably contrived to do what cars are standardly needed and used to do – namely, transport persons and things from one location to another in a particular manner. A motorcycle does not count as a car because it is not reasonably contrived to do what cars are needed and used to do. In contrast, a car with a broken engine nonetheless counts as a car if it can be repaired so as to reenable it to do what cars are standardly needed and used to do. However, if not, it counts as totaled and counts as a car only in the attenuated sense that a completely disassembled car or toy car counts as one. For more discussion of the nature of artifacts, see Kenneth Einar Himma, *Coercion and the Nature of Law* (Oxford University Press, 2020), ch. 4.

It is important to note that someone can have practical authority over a subject who always complies – provided that she is not *necessarily* preinclined to do what the authority tells her to do independently of being told to do it. *P* can count as having practical authority only over subjects who are *potentially recalcitrant* in the sense that they *can be* initially inclined to do otherwise but who would nevertheless comply enough in those instances to enable *P* to minimally achieve the ends *P* seeks to achieve by directing their behavior.

The second is that *P* counts as having practical authority over *Q* only if *P*'s tellings are sufficiently efficacious in *inducing Q*'s compliance to enable *P* to minimally achieve the ends she directs *Q*'s behavior to achieve. This claim mirrors the efficacy condition for law, as it should, given that law is a conspicuous instance of authoritative guidance. But it is important to note that this claim entails that subjects regard authoritative tellings as having normative force and that authoritative tellings sometimes induce compliance in subjects when initially undecided about what to do.

Both claims follow straightforwardly from the idea that a telling counts as authoritative with respect to *Q* only if made by someone who has the power of will-imposition over what *Q* does (i.e., claim (6) above). To impose one's will is, as *Merriam-Webster* defines the locution, to "force other people to do what one wants."[28] The claim that *P* has the power to *force Q* to do what *P* directs *Q* to do entails that *Q* acquiesces by doing what *P* has *forced Q* to do *and* that *P*'s tellings are at least minimally efficacious in inducing *Q*'s compliance.

The only other plausible candidate for a constitutive property of authoritative telling that I can think of is expressed by the Exclusionary Thesis. The Exclusionary Thesis cannot be inferred from claim (6), as should be clear. Nor, as was discussed above in Section 4.2 and will be discussed in more detail below in Section 14, does the Exclusionary Thesis purport to describe a constitutive property of authoritative guidance. But, either way, because I think the Exclusionary Thesis is false, I will attempt a refutation of it in Section 14.

Obviously, I cannot conclusively rule out there being other plausible candidates for constitutive properties of authoritative tellings, but this much is clear: given that claims (1) through (7) express conceptual truisms about the nature of authoritative guidance, any other claims that describe constitutive properties of authoritative tellings must be consistent with those claims. Further, assuming that I succeed in deriving the Sanctions Thesis from these truisms, any other candidates for constitutive properties of authoritative tellings must also be consistent with the Sanctions Thesis.

---

[28] www.merriam-webster.com/dictionary/impose%20one's%20will. *Cambridge* defines the usage of the term *impose* as "to officially force a rule, tax, punishment, etc. to be obeyed or received." https://dictionary.cambridge.org/us/dictionary/english/impose.

PART III CLAIMS (1) THROUGH (7) AND THE SANCTIONS THESIS

7 Practical Authority as Telling People What to Do

Authoritative guidance is distinguished from other forms of guidance in that its point is to guide behavior by telling subjects what they *must* do – as opposed to what they merely *should* do. A high-school guidance counselor might well have epistemic authority on what students should do and might invoke the corresponding expertise to advise them. But her prescriptions, no matter how couched ("you simply must apply to university"), do not count as authoritative because a guidance counselor lacks practical authority over students.

Tellings assert that something must be done and thus express, or purport to express, content that constitutes a *requirement*. A prescription that some act s should be done counts as telling some set S of subjects what to do only if (a) it is mandatory in the sense it requires, or purports to require, members of S to do s, and (b) it has a source in some class of agents T, such as a court or legislature, that is not identical with S, to which we can aptly attribute actions and which thus constitutes a composite, or collective, agent.[29] While the sets S and T can be singletons (i.e., consist of only one member), they cannot be identical because no one can do something that counts as telling oneself what to do.

The requirement is created by the telling. Though there might be other prescriptions that require the same act, a telling creates a requirement of a different kind: a law requiring an act antecedently required by morality creates a legal requirement distinct from the moral requirement; a conventional norm requiring an act that is antecedently required by law *and* morality creates a conventional requirement distinct from the legal and moral requirements; and so on.

One common response to a telling issued by someone who does not *obviously* have authority over the recipient challenges her ability to enforce it – "or what?" Though phrased as a question, "or what?" insinuates, and aggressively so, that there is nothing that the utterer can do to enforce the telling and hence denies that the subject must do what the telling says she must do. The aptness of the "or what?" response indicates that we conceive of tellings as inherently bundled with an implicit "do it, or else" and hence assumes that content counts as a telling partly in virtue of expressing a credible threat of enforcement.[30]

---

[29] For this reason, mandatory conventional norms count as defining requirements but do not count as tellings if the set of persons establishing the conventional norm is identical with the set of persons whose behavior is governed by the norm.

[30] I will use the term *enforcement* here even though it might be that only authoritative tellings are correctly characterized as *enforced* because there is no more general term capturing the idea. Though I could express the matter in terms of something *resembling* enforcement, there is no

A more aggressive response to a presumptively inappropriate telling is to say to its utterer "make me."[31] Like the "or what?" response, "make me" does not use fighting words but is likely to be construed as a threat. In particular, it promises that any attempt to enforce the telling will be met with force that suffices not just to defend against it but also to deter any future transgressions. As is true of the first response, the "make me" response assumes that every utterance that counts as a *telling* is backed by detriment.

Another common response to such tellings is to say, "you're not my mother/ father." This assumes that parents are emblematic of practical authority and denies that the utterer of the telling has the authority assumed by its utterance: in essence, this response expresses that, unlike one's parents, the utterer of the telling lacks practical authority over the person to whom the telling is directed.

It should be noted that the assumption that parental authority counts as an instance of practical authority is problematic. The concern here is that the phrase *parental authority* is often used to apply to children who have not developed enough competence to count, on our moral and legal practices, as subject to practical authority. Though it is true, of course, that parents frequently have to tell their young children what to do, this does not entail they have practical authority over their children – any more than the fact a robber tells her victim what to do entails she has practical authority over her victim. What is thought to be practical authority over children is hence better understood as a species of custodial authority that limits the interference of *other* persons in matters involving a child until she reaches the age of majority or is emancipated by a court.

There are just two ways to interpret the "you're not my mother/father" response; but neither is as aggressive as "or what?" or "make me" because neither invites a teller to enforce the telling nor threatens retaliation if she tries to do so. On the first, it denies that the teller, unlike the parents of a young child, has the *causal* ability to enforce a telling with enough detriment to induce its recipient to comply, because the putative subject can resist whatever force the teller can muster. However, to the extent that this interpretation expresses resistance, it is more accurately described as *promising defense* than as *threatening aggression*.[32] On the second, it denies that the teller, unlike the recipient's

---

need to do so once the reader is aware of the issue. To *enforce* a telling, as I use the term, is simply to impose whatever detriment there is that backs it.

[31] Although framed as an imperative, "make me" does not count as a telling because the point of the response is not to require the utterer to enforce her telling. The point is to get the utterer to back off.

[32] Insofar as Q is willing and able to resist attempts on the part of P to enforce a telling, the "you're not my mother/father" response distinguishes P from Q's parents, whose enforcement efforts Q would not resist. Q's posture towards P is different from that towards her parents in the following way: on the one hand, Q is both willing and able to resist P's efforts to enforce her

parents, has the needed *permission* to enforce her tellings – and threatens neither resistance nor aggression.

But the point, on each interpretation, is to call attention to the fact that the utterer lacks a capacity of some kind, whether causal or norm-governed, to punish noncompliance with disciplinary force; it is not to call attention to the fact the utterer lacks parental or custodial authority over a subject, which is never in question except in truly unusual circumstances that do not matter here.[33] The naturalness of this response, like the others, thus supports the claim it is a necessary condition for P to have *authority* over Q that P has a norm-governed capacity to enforce her tellings against Q.

This is true of another response that does the same work done by "you're not my mother/father" but without implicating the flawed notion of parental authority: the "you're not the boss of me" response denies that the teller has practical authority over the recipient on the ground the teller lacks the causal ability or requisite permission to enforce the telling. Someone counts as a *boss* in an organization partly in virtue of being able to enforce her tellings with detriment reasonably contrived to deter enough noncompliance to enable her to minimally achieve her ends. Such detriment, in the case of a lawful enterprise, might consist in having one's job terminated but, in the case of an organized criminal gang, might consist in having one's entire future terminated. In both cases, the "you're not the boss of me" response, like the others, repudiates the authority of an utterer by denying that she has the requisite capacity to enforce it.

Accordingly, all these responses assume that, to count as a telling, a piece of content must be backed by a threat of detriment that is reasonably contrived to induce compliance in someone not initially inclined to do what the putative telling requires. Since any content that counts as an authoritative telling also counts as a telling, the Sanctions Thesis follows trivially.

8 Practical Authority as a Source of Reasons to Comply

Our conceptual and nonconceptual practices assume that authoritative guidance is normative in the following sense: any telling that counts as authoritative gives rise to a reason to do what it requires. If a police officer, employer, or anyone else with practical authority directs you to do something within the scope of her

---

telling; on the other, though Q might be able to resist her parents, she is unwilling to do so. Q might believe her parents' demands are unfair but will comply to placate them or accept whatever detriment her parents have decided to impose to punish noncompliance.

[33] One difference between custodial authority and practical authority is that someone with custodial authority over Q exercises that authority by making decisions for Q to ensure Q's interests are adequately protected in cases where Q lacks the capacity to protect them – and not by telling Q what to do. Custodial authority applies only where the subject lacks either the competence or freedom (in the case of incarceration) to make decisions for herself.

authority to direct you to do, you have a reason to do it. That reason may be defeated by other reasons. However, you have a reason to do it because someone with authority to tell you to do it has told you to do it. Authoritative guidance is thus *conceptually normative* in the sense that authoritative tellings give rise, as a matter of conceptual necessity, to reasons that are source-based – or, as the matter is typically put, "content-independent" – because those reasons derive from the source of the telling and not its content.

8.1 Authoritative Guidance as Giving Rise to Objective Reasons

The propositions constituting the reasons to comply count as *objective* insofar as objective standards of practical reasoning require rational self-interested agents to consider them in their decision-making about what ought to be done. The capacity of authoritative guidance to generate subjective reasons (i.e., propositions that *actually* function as reasons in the minds of a subject, as a descriptive matter of fact) is, then, grounded in its capacity to generate objective reasons (i.e., propositions that *should* function as reasons in the minds of subjects, as a normative matter of practical reasoning). Whether a person counts as rational hence depends on whether her deliberations about what she should do minimally conform to what we take to be objective standards of practical reasoning.

8.2 Motivating, Justifying, and Explanatory Reasons

Practical reasons can be distinguished on the basis of how they support an act. A *motivating reason* to do s̲ is a proposition that a subject regards, or should regard, as motivating her to do s̲ and that inclines, or should incline, her to do it. Motivating reasons function to incline – and thus to motivate – subjects to do what they are motivating reasons to do.[34] A *justifying* reason to do s̲ is a proposition that some subject views, or should view, as justifying her in doing s̲ under a system of standards that antecedently governs her acts.[35] Justifying reasons function to justify the subject in doing what some norm requires or permits her to do *under the same normative system to which the norm belongs*. These systems include both law and morality.

Theorists sometimes distinguish a class of explanatory reasons, which explain why someone did something, but these are just descriptive historical

---

[34] To motivate someone to do *a̲* is to incline her to do *a̲* by giving her a reason to do it. As *Merriam-Webster* defines it, a *motive* is "something (such as a need or desire) that causes a person to act."

[35] Justifying reasons are sometimes referred to as *normative* reasons. See, e.g., David McNaughton and Piers Rawling, "Motivating Reasons and Normative Reasons," in Daniel Star (ed.), *The Oxford Handbook of Reasons and Normativity* (Oxford University Press, 2018), pp. 171–196. I have chosen this nomenclature to eliminate ambiguity, such as occurs when some people use *normative* to refer only to objective reasons and others use it to refer only to justifying reasons.

reports of what motivating reasons figured into a subject's decisions to do what she did. Otherwise put, an explanatory reason is a proposition that figured into the subject's *past reasoning* about what she should do and is hence, in essence, just a description of her (subjective) reasons for having done something.[36] Although recourse to such reports can help us to ascertain whether something some subject did *was* justified, explanatory reasons do not function to guide conduct – and are hence irrelevant with respect to how practical authority guides behavior by giving rise to reasons to comply.

The relevant reasons *to comply* are motivating reasons. Practical authority attempts to induce compliance by motivating it – and not by justifying it. The function of a law that prohibits murder is to generate a new reason that motivates subjects to abstain from murder in cases where the preexisting moral reasons do not succeed in inducing them to abstain; law subjects have *never* needed to *legally* justify not killing people.[37] A mandatory legal norm might also provide justifying reasons that justify an act *under the law*. However, such norms do so only with respect to two classes of act: (i) acts falling under exceptions to legal norms that govern *unofficial* behavior (e.g., those allowing self-defense) and (ii) acts falling under legal norms that govern *official* behavior (e.g., those authorizing the court to enforce a telling by imposing a sanction). While it is true that one can have a motivating reason to act in a manner that is justified under the law, this is a different matter.

Either way, if authoritative tellings necessarily give rise to reasons to comply, then those reasons are objective and motivating in character. Authoritative guidance attempts to induce compliance by manufacturing an incentive to comply – in the form, as we will see, of a disincentive to disobedience – that is reasonably contrived, and therefore reasonably likely, to motivate rationally competent self-interested subjects like us to comply.

8.3 Three Irreducible Sources of Value and Normative Force

We cannot explain how authoritative tellings create objective motivating reasons to comply without identifying the source of value that endows them with what normative force they have. The actions of rationally self-interested

---

[36] See Maria Alvarez and Jonathan Way, "Reasons for Action: Justification, Motivation, and Explanation," in Edward N. Zalta and Uri Nodelman (eds.), *The Stanford Encyclopedia of Philosophy* (Fall 2024 edition), https://plato.stanford.edu/archives/fall2024/entries/reasons-just-vs-expl/.

[37] Notice that there is never any need to justify a behavior within a system unless it presumptively conflicts with some existing norm of that system. It would hence make no sense to enact a law prohibiting murder for the purpose of abstaining from murder because there was no preexisting legal norm that required subjects to commit murder. I am grateful to Pablo Ariel Rapetti for making me aware of the need to address this point.

subjects like us are motivated by three kinds of considerations that cannot be reduced to other more basic considerations that we regard as having value: these pertain to whether an action (1) satisfies morality; (2) promotes self-interest; or (3) results in beauty.[38] These three considerations correspond to three sources of value that endow any prescription with what normative force it is, or should be, regarded as having.[39]

It is not just happenstance that we are motivated by values from these sources. Self-interested subjects like us are not likely to survive, much less thrive, in worlds like ours if we are not motivated by each of these irreducible values. Things will not go well for people unmoved by aesthetic value, because it is difficult to have satisfying relationships without caring about beauty and the various media through which it is expressed, like films, novels, and music. But things will go catastrophically badly for people who are unmoved by moral or, assuming this is even nomologically possible for beings hardwired like us, prudential value – so much so that the mental health of someone who does not care at all about these two types of value is suspect for that reason.[40]

The conceptual normativity of authoritative guidance must ultimately be explained in terms of objective motivating reasons derived from these sources of value. Authoritative tellings are equipped to guide our behavior only if reasonably contrived to make a practical difference in what rationally competent self-interested subjects like us decide to do. But a telling can make such a practical difference *only* by giving rise to something that rationally competent subjects like us are reasonably likely to regard as a motivating reason to comply because we should regard it as a motivating reason to comply. Given that these three kinds of value exhaust the considerations that rationally competent

---

[38] It is generally assumed that moral and prudential values are the only two irreducible sources of normativity. See, e.g., Roger Crisp, "Prudential and Moral Reasons," in Daniel Star (ed.), *The Oxford Handbook of Reasons and Normativity* (Oxford University Press, 2018), pp. 800–820. While I am convinced altruistic value can be explained wholly in terms of moral and prudential values, our nonconceptual practices appear to entail that beauty is intrinsically and thus irreducibly valuable. "Beauty for its own sake," as the slogan goes. But nothing of importance here turns on this.

[39] It is true that we value many things – for example, truth, friendship, art, humor. But such value is ultimately derived from at least one of these irreducible sources of value. We value friendship for a number of prudential and moral reasons. We value art for prudential and aesthetic reasons. While one might think that there are other irreducible sources of value, it is clear that any such sources are not relevant in explicating the conceptual normativity of authoritative guidance.

[40] It is not nomologically possible for beings like us to be indifferent about our prudential interests. Although one might think that people who end their lives are not motivated by prudential interests, this is mistaken; in all but the most unusual cases, they are motivated to end what they experience as unbearable pain – emotional in the case of depression and physical in the case of an excruciating terminal illness. I trust it is nomologically possible for us to subordinate our interests to the greater good. But that does not involve indifference to what we take to be in our own interests.

subjects like us are reasonably likely to treat as reasons to comply because we should treat them as reasons to comply, the conceptual normativity of authoritative guidance must be explained in terms of these three values.

Authoritative guidance is equipped to guide behavior, then, only if its tellings give rise, by nature, to objective motivating reasons from at least one of these three basic sources because only reasons from such sources are sufficiently likely to induce compliance in self-interested subjects who count as rationally competent in virtue of deliberating in a manner minimally responsive to what we converge in thinking are objective standards of epistemic and practical reasoning.

It is clear that an authoritative telling *need not* create an objective moral or aesthetic motivating reason. It may be true that the tellings of a legitimate legal system, which count as authoritative in virtue of counting as law, necessarily give rise to objective *moral* reasons to comply. But there is nothing in just the practices constituting a normative system as one of law that entails that every legal system is morally legitimate; history is replete, after all, with instances of legal systems that are unconscionably wicked. While, moreover, there is considerable beauty in the breadth, depth, and coherence of our legal practices, there is nothing in them even remotely contrived to give rise to aesthetic reasons to do what law requires – assuming this counterintuitive notion is even coherent.

The only way, then, to explain the conceptual normativity of authoritative guidance is in terms of its capacity to create something that subjects are plausibly presumed to regard as a prudential motivating reason to comply because subjects should regard it as such. Since (1) any telling that counts as authoritative gives rise to an objective motivating reason to comply, (2) any proposition that counts as a motivating reason to do something expresses a value from one of these basic sources, and (3) there can be authoritative tellings that give rise to neither objective moral nor aesthetic motivating reasons, it follows that any telling that counts as authoritative gives rise to an objective *prudential* motivating reason to do as it requires. Authoritative tellings, then, give rise to objective prudential motivating reasons to comply, as a matter of conceptual necessity.

It might be true that an authoritative telling can create objective motivating reasons expressing value from more than one of these basic sources of value; but this much is clear: the *conceptual* normativity of any particular species of normative system can be explained only in terms of its *constitutive* properties – that is, those *constituting* a norm as a member of that system. If these constitutive properties give rise to an objective motivating reason from one source in even one instance, they *must* do so in *every* instance; if they *do not* give rise to an objective motivating reason from that source in one instance, they *cannot* do so in *any* instance.

8.4 Two Kinds of Reason-Giving: Robust and Triggering

We cannot explain how authoritative guidance gives rise, by nature, to objective motivating reasons to comply without considering David Enoch's important distinction between two kinds of reason-giving: robust and triggering. Robust reason-giving involves the creation of a novel reason – that is, one that did not preexist the norm. Reason-giving by triggering, in contrast, involves altering the descriptive nonnormative facts to implicate the applicability of a preexisting reason that was not previously applicable.[41]

It is not clear that human beings can create practical reasons that have never existed; nor is it clear what we would have to do to create such reasons. While Enoch suggests that requests give rise to reasons to comply in the robust sense, it strikes me as more plausible to think that requests can give rise to reasons only by triggering preexisting prudential and moral reasons; after all, it is prudentially and morally good, all else being equal, to satisfy reasonable requests. Doing favors is presumed to be good – and, within reason, rightly so.

Either way, it is clear that authoritative tellings can give rise to objective motivating reasons only by triggering preexisting reasons from one of the sources described in Section 8.3. Since, as we have seen, there are just three basic irreducible sources of value, the only reasons that an authoritative telling can give rise to must express a value from at least one of these sources. Further, since these value-sources preexist the utterance of a telling, the only reasons that an authoritative telling can give rise to must likewise preexist the telling. Accordingly, an authoritative telling can give rise to an objective motivating reason only by triggering a preexisting reason from one of these sources.

Given that there can be tellings requiring wicked acts that count as authoritative, on our descriptive usage of the term, and that hence do not trigger preexisting *moral* reasons, the only reason-giving capacity plausibly attributed to the nature of authority is the capacity to trigger preexisting objective *prudential* motivating reasons. If the only irreducible kind of practical reason to which an authoritative telling gives rise, by nature, is prudential, then an authoritative telling can guide behavior only by triggering the application of some preexisting objective motivating prudential reason that was inapplicable before its issuance.

8.5 How Authoritative Tellings Trigger Prudential Reasons to Comply: The Sanctions Thesis

Only the Sanctions Thesis explains how authoritative tellings trigger preexisting objective motivating prudential reasons to comply as a matter of conceptual

---

[41] David Enoch, "Reason-Giving and the Law," in Leslie Green and Brian Leiter (eds.), *Oxford Studies in Philosophy of Law: Volume 1* (Oxford University Press, 2011), pp. 1–38.

necessity. A threat of detriment that backs a telling triggers a prudential reason to comply as a means of avoiding the detriment. Since rewards cannot motivate compliance by *deterring* noncompliance, the Sanctions Thesis uniquely explains what equips authoritative guidance, by nature, to deter enough non-compliance to enable the authority to minimally achieve the ends she seeks to achieve by telling subjects what they must do. Although there may be many considerations a particular subject regards, as a purely contingent matter, as other kinds of reason, the only constitutive property of an authoritative telling that is reasonably contrived – and therefore equipped by nature – to trigger an objective motivating prudential reason to comply is that it is backed by a threat of detriment that constitutes a sanction. Only the Sanctions Thesis, then, has the resources to explain the conceptual normativity of authoritative guidance.

9 Practical Authority as a Personal Relationship

Authority relations can hold only among beings that resemble us in ways that explain why we standardly need and use authoritative guidance to do what we standardly need and use it to do. Authoritative guidance is efficacious because there is something about *it* equipped to do what we need and use *it* to do. But it is equipped to do what we need and use it to do only because there is something about *us* that is responsive to the constitutive mechanisms it deploys to do these things.[42]

What explains why we are responsive to these mechanisms, in part, is that we have psychological features that enable us to have relationships that count as personal with other beings with these features. Authority relations cannot obtain among impersonal things like plants, bacteria, and boxes, because authority is neither needed nor able to do among them what it is needed and able to do among us. Only beings who count as personal in virtue of instantiating certain psychological properties can have or be subject to practical authority, because only beings with these properties can have the kind of personal relationship that is defined by the authority relation.

That the authority relation is a personal relationship can be seen from the etymology of the word. The term *authority* includes *author* as its root, and its inclusion is not a matter of chance. *Author*ities are *authors* of tellings that count as *author*itative, and *authors* count as personal in virtue of being able to do something that constitutes *author*ing content – authoring being done in this case

---

[42] Authoritative guidance resembles penicillin in this respect: penicillin works because it is equipped to do what we need and use it to. However, it is equipped to do these things only because there is something about us that makes us responsive to the mechanisms it deploys to do those things. What explains why authoritative guidance and penicillin work has as much to do with facts about *us* as with facts about *them*.

for persons who comprise an audience of sorts in virtue of being subject to the tellings of the authoring authority.[43] The issue is to explain the sense in which the authority relation counts as a *personal* relationship that can obtain only among personal beings.

The relevant use of *personal* is defined in terms of the capacity for a particular kind of awareness: *Oxford* defines the usage as "existing as an entity with self-awareness, not as an abstraction or an impersonal force," whereas *Merriam-Webster* defines it as "being ... self-conscious."[44] Two subjects can count as personal and hence as able to have a relationship that counts as personal only if each is conscious not only in the sense of being brutely aware – aware simpliciter – but also in the sense of being aware one is aware. Brute consciousness is not enough to constitute two beings as able to stand in the authority relation; in addition, two subjects can stand in an authority relation only if each is aware of being aware – or, as the definitions put the matter, each is self-aware or self-conscious.[45]

What being aware one is aware amounts to is not clear;[46] however, it involves being aware that one is distinct from at least one other thing. Self-awareness in this sense is basic, because it need not involve being aware of any material entities: even if none of my sense perceptions is veridical because all are induced by some Cartesian deceiver, I count as self-aware in virtue of being aware I am distinct from those perceptions. Indeed, a being can be self-aware in this fundamental sense without having any sense organs at all.

That said, even these fleshed-out definitions lack the resources to fully explain how something that counts as personal can stand in the authority relation because one being can have authority over another only if each is aware *of the other*. These reports of the meaning of the term *personal* do not *assert* that a being must have the capacity for other-awareness to count as

---

[43] It would be nonstandard to describe the act of writing something *not* intended for an audience, like a diary, as *authoring*. When a diary is published, its creator counts as an author and its creation constitutes an act of authoring. But it is arguable that her writing counts as authoring only if she consents or does not object to its being published.

[44] www.oed.com/dictionary/personal_adj?tab=meaning_and_use#30954873; www.merriam-web ster.com/dictionary/personal.

[45] The relevant usage of *self-conscious* should not be construed as referring to the painful state associated with debilitating shyness. *Merriam-Webster* defines this latter use as "uncomfortably conscious of oneself as an object of observation of others" and defines the usage above as "conscious of one's own acts or states as belonging in oneself: aware of oneself as an individual." www.merriam-webster.com/dictionary/self-conscious.

[46] It cannot refer to an awareness of being aware if that requires some mysterious capacity for second-order awareness, *awareness* being construed in the same way in both instances. While I can grasp, apprehend, or understand I am aware, this is a different matter. Self-awareness in this respect implicates a cognitive ability – and not some metaphysically queer faculty for brute higher-order awareness that is distinct from awareness simpliciter.

personal. But that is because they assume that a capacity for self-awareness defines a corresponding capacity for other-awareness. What constitutes a dog as personal is, for instance, that she is aware of other beings who likewise count as personal, which enables her to have relationships with them. A being counts as personal, then, only if she is capable of having relationships that count as personal. The concept of personal, then, is inherently relational.

A relationship counts as personal in virtue of being communicative in character. A personal relationship is constituted by a series of mutually responsive *actions*: part of what enables a human being and dog to have a personal relationship is that they can *do* things together; a person can play fetch with a dog only if both can perform the acts needed to play the game and possess something like an understanding of how to play it.[47] But they can do these things together only to the extent their interaction communicates to each other that a game is being played. To count as personal, then, a being must have the capacity to communicate in some manner with other personal beings.

The capacity for communicative agency is, of course, central to our attributions of practical authority and authoritativeness. Communication performs a function essential to authoritative guidance because content does not constitute a telling unless communicated to subjects: insofar as (1) the basic/conceptual point/function of practical authority is to tell subjects what to do and (2) something must have the ability to perform the basic/conceptual point/function of practical authority to count as having practical authority over others, one being can count as having practical authority over another being only if each is capable of communicative agency and can exercise it through communicative acts that are understood by the other.

The idea that the authority relation can hold only among subjects who count as personal in virtue of possessing these psychological features, by itself, tells us nothing more exciting than that the Sanctions Thesis *could* be true. However, that accomplishes nothing, because all this shows is that the Sanctions Thesis is *coherent* (that is, not self-contradictory). The problem is that just knowing P and Q are self-aware, other-aware, and capable of actions that are reasonably contrived to communicate content says nothing about whether they can impose or experience something that counts as detriment. For that reason, merely knowing two beings have these properties entails nothing about whether they

---

[47] I say have "something like an understanding" because it is unclear whether only rational beings are properly described as *understanding* content. Though we commonly attribute a rudimentary capacity of understanding to dogs, it is unclear whether the assumptions conditioning our ordinary attributions of understanding entail that only beings with linguistic capacities, lacking in dogs, can understand content.

can induce someone to comply by threatening detriment or be induced to comply as a means of avoiding its imposition.

Either way, it is clear that only beings who are self- and other-aware are responsive to threats of detriment because only such beings can grasp a threat or experience something as detriment. However, the idea that those who have or are subject to authority are capable of communicative agency partly in virtue of being self- and other-aware, by itself, does not entail that the constitutive properties of authoritative guidance include threats of detriment. The claim that only personal beings can be induced to act by a threat tells us nothing, then, about whether the constitutive mechanism through which practical authority tries to induce compliance is by deploying such threats.

To dispel any potential confusion about the implications of this analysis, it would be helpful to consider the relationship between the concept of personal and the concept of a person as this latter concept figures into debates about the morality of abortion. First, the concept of personal is purely descriptive in the sense that all its constitutive properties are factually descriptive, as was discussed above. In contrast, the concept of a person is a *thick* concept that has morally evaluative *and* factually descriptive elements. That a being counts as a person, on this thick usage, entails that it has a special moral status which endows it with a right to life equal in strength to that held by every other being that counts as a person.

Second, the two concepts are logically independent.[48] It is not, to begin, a sufficient condition for a being to count as a person, on this usage, that it counts as *personal,* on this descriptive usage. Dogs count as personal on this usage but not as persons on this morally thick usage. This does not *imply* that dogs do not have the same moral rights as persons – although this latter claim is not absurd. However, they do not count as persons. Conversely, it is not a necessary condition for a being to count as a person on this thick usage that it counts as personal. Abortion rights opponents believe that human fetuses count as persons from the moment of conception. Regardless of whether this claim is true, it is clear that human fetuses do not count as *personal* from the moment of conception, because they do not become brutely conscious until twenty-four weeks of gestational development. In consequence, they lack *all* of the constitutive properties needed to count as personal.[49]

---

[48] One might think that this simply follows from claims about the impossibility of deducing is-statements from ought-statements and the impossibility of deducing ought-statements from is-statements. However, the concept of a person is a thick concept that has both descriptive and morally evaluative elements. Descriptive claims can be deduced from claims involving thick concepts. For instance, the descriptive claim that P killed Q is implied by the claim that P murdered Q because the concept of murder is thick in virtue of having both descriptive and morally evaluative elements.

[49] See, e.g., Hugo Lagercrantz, "The Emergence of Consciousness: Science and Ethics," *Seminars in Fetal and Natal Development*, vol. 17, no. 5 (2014), 300–305.

10 Practical Authority as Rational

Authoritative guidance is successful in guiding our conduct because it is properly equipped to do what we standardly need and use it to do; but, as discussed in Section 9, it is equipped to do what we need and use it to do only because we have psychological features that make *us* responsive to the constitutive mechanisms that authoritative guidance deploys to do all of these things. What explains why these mechanisms are successful in doing what we need and use them to do in the circumstances in which we deploy them has as much to do with facts about us as it does with facts about those mechanisms.

There are two facts about us that help to explain why authoritative guidance, as we conceive it, is equipped to do what we standardly need and use it to do. The first, discussed in Section 9, is that we possess self-awareness, other-awareness, and communicative agency, which constitutes us as personal. The second, discussed in this section, is that we make decisions about what to believe and do in a manner minimally responsive to what we believe are objective standards of epistemic and practical reasoning, which constitutes us as rationally competent.

The claim that only rationally competent beings can be *subject* to practical authority is uncontentious. A personal being can stand in the authority relation as subject only if she is *capable* of being rationally induced to do something she is not initially inclined to do.[50] Someone *psychologically incapable* of being rationally induced to do something she is not initially inclined to do cannot be told what to do except in the uninteresting sense that she can be the intended recipient of an utterance that expresses, or purports to express, a telling. The most basic point of any telling, authoritative or not, is to guide behavior. But only the behavior of personal beings who can be rationally induced to comply can be efficaciously guided.[51]

The claim that only rationally competent beings can *have* practical authority is less obvious but also true. A personal being can stand in the authority relation as authority only if she has intelligible ends and can discern what others need to do in order for her to achieve those ends. The tellings of someone utterly lacking this ability would be arbitrary, inconsistent, and hence incapable of guiding behavior as a means of achieving those ends. Only a person with intelligible

---

[50] Rational inducement involves persuading someone to believe/do something by convincing her that she has winning reasons to believe/do it.

[51] It is helpful to note that the claim that someone is conclusively – as opposed to necessarily – committed to doing what an authority tells her to do is *consistent* with the claim she is capable of being rationally induced to do what she is not initially inclined to do. I take myself to be conclusively committed to not killing people, but this doesn't imply that I am psychologically incapable of murder. As the joke goes, I just haven't met the right victim yet.

ends who can ascertain how the behavior of others contributes to achieving them can guide the behavior of someone else.

Although the topic of rationality has generated a large philosophical literature, it is almost exclusively concerned with articulating norms of epistemic and practical reasoning, rather than with explicating the nature of rationality. While these theories are sometimes expressed in terms of claims about the relationship between reasons and norms,[52] they are normative theories that explain how rationally competent beings should reason, rather than descriptive theories that articulate the conditions that must be met to count as rational.[53]

Theorists seem to assume that the nature of rationality can be adequately explicated simply by identifying the right principles of reasoning. While Robert Nozick, for instance, entitled his book on the topic *The Nature of Rationality*, there is nothing in that volume that even purports to be a conceptual analysis of the sort I attempt in this section. As Nozick describes his objectives in the book:

> We shall reformulate current decision theory to include the symbolic meaning of actions, propose a new rule of rational decision (that of maximizing decision-value), and then proceed to trace the implications of this rule for the Prisoner's Dilemma and for Newcomb's Problem. . . . I also shall explore the scope and limits of instrumental rationality, the effective and efficient pursuit of given goals . . .[54]

By its own terms, then, the book is concerned to articulate objective standards of rationality as they apply to difficult issues of reasoning. While this account may succeed in improving our understanding of the norms governing practical reasoning, it tells us nothing about the nature of rationality because it assumes our grasp of the concept is satisfactory.

---

[52] Raz's *Practical Reason and Norms* is best understood as a theory of rationality that takes the shape of a descriptive analysis of the concept of a *norm* together with a normative theory of how norms should function in practical reasoning. As he describes his goal in the introduction: "This is a study in the theory of norms. . . . The key concept for the explanation of norms is that of reasons for action. . . . The central thesis of the book is that some kinds of rules (categorical and permissive rules) are reasons for action of a special type, and other rules (power-conferring rules) are logically related to such reasons." Ibid., 9. Since the concept of a norm is clearly different from that of a reason, it is more accurate to say that norms *give rise to* reasons than that norms *are* reasons. But since Raz takes himself to be advancing a novel thesis about the kinds of reasons he identifies with certain norms, he is not plausibly construed as making descriptive claims about the nature of rationality and is best construed as making normative claims about how we should reason.

[53] It is worth noting here that the most comprehensive online resource in philosophy, *Stanford Encyclopedia of Philosophy*, does not include an entry devoted to the nature of rationality. That omission strikes me as both notable and problematic.

[54] Robert Nozick, *The Nature of Rationality* (Princeton University Press, 1993). A quick perusal of the contents confirms this.

That might be right, but it would nonetheless be helpful to say a bit about the nature of rationality. *Collins* defines the term *rational* as meaning "able to make decisions based on intelligent thinking rather than on emotion," whereas *Merriam-Webster* defines it as meaning "having reason or understanding."[55] Rationality, on each definition, requires the power of reason.

The power of reason is constituted by a capacity to process propositional content in a manner that minimally satisfies norms of reasoning.[56] *Oxford* defines *reason* as meaning "[t]he power of the mind to think and form valid judgements by a process of *logic*,"[57] while *Merriam-Webster* defines it as meaning "the power of comprehending, inferring, or *thinking* especially in *orderly* rational ways."[58]

Although these definitions of *reason* assume that the power of reason comes with the capacity to satisfy these standards, they do not assume the relevant mental processes always do so. Rather, they refer to, as *Collins* expresses it, "the *ability* that people have to think and to make *sensible* judgments."[59] Given that a judgment can count as *sensible* without optimally satisfying these standards, the power of reason should be understood as just the *ability* to think about what one should believe/do in a manner that is minimally responsive to what we converge in believing are objective standards of logic and orderly thinking.

While the relevant notion of a capacity picks out an ability that is causal in nature, it does not suffice to constitute someone as rational that she has a causal ability to reason. The claim that *P* has such an ability tells us no more than that her body has the necessary hardware in the form of a brain that has enough computing power to enable *P* to reason. While instantiating this ability is a necessary condition to count as rationally competent, it is not a sufficient condition.

To count as rationally competent, *P* must also exercise this *ability* to reason in a manner that is minimally responsive to standards of reasoning. There are

---

[55] www.collinsdictionary.com/dictionary/english/rational; www.merriam-webster.com/dictionary/rational.

[56] The inference rules of any system of logic operate only on propositions: the rule *modus ponens* permits the inference of a proposition appearing as the consequent of a conditional from that conditional and the proposition appearing as its antecedent; *universal instantiation* permits the inference of the proposition that some given entity has a property from the proposition that every entity has that property; and so on. While one can reason about whether one part of a sentence expressing a proposition can be replaced with something else in a manner that preserves its truth value, one must nonetheless reason with propositions to reach a justified conclusion on this issue.

[57] www.oed.com/dictionary/reason_n1?tab=meaning_and_use#26881284 (emphasis added).

[58] www.merriam-webster.com/dictionary/reason (emphasis added).

[59] www.collinsdictionary.com/us/dictionary/english/reason (emphasis added). *Collins* defines *sensible* as "actions or decisions … based on reasons rather than emotions." www.collinsdictionary.com/dictionary/english/sensible. As should be clear, a decision can be based on reasons without satisfying the relevant standards of epistemic or practical rationality.

many persons regarded as incompetent despite possessing the nomologically requisite hardware: the disabilities associated with mental illnesses like schizophrenia can be so bad that afflicted persons are deemed not competent – despite the fact that their brains might still have the requisite computing power. Though there are physical causes impairing the operation of the brain in these unfortunate cases, this is consistent with its instantiating the causal capacity to do what brains normally do.[60]

And the vast majority of our day-to-day decisions are obviously responsive to these standards: when we need groceries, we go to the market to buy them; when we need gas, we go to the gas station to fill the tank; when we decide to be doctors, we apply to medical school; etc. Truly worrisome problems of poor decision-making occur only at the margins: while these problems might happen with sufficient frequency to lead one to doubt we count as rational in some ideal, immodest sense,[61] the nature of rationality, as it is constructed by our conceptual practices, defines a comparatively low bar.

Rationality, as that concept figures into ordinary attributions of authoritativeness, requires competence in epistemic *and* practical reasoning. Only personal beings who are epistemically rational count as practically rational: one can deliberate about what to do in a manner minimally responsive to standards of *practical* reasoning only to the extent that one's beliefs are formed in a manner minimally responsive to standards of *epistemic* reasoning. It is not just that the standards of practical reasoning include the logical norms that function as standards of epistemic rationality; it is, further, that one cannot arrive at justified *decisions* about what to *do* without processing evidence for claims that function as premises in lines of reasoning concerned with arriving at justified *beliefs* about what to do.

But, in addition, an attribution of rationality presupposes that the subject's beliefs and acts are at least sometimes conditioned by her reasoning. Someone utterly infallible about what ought to be believed or done does not count as rational if her reasoning never conditions her beliefs or acts. It is not enough to constitute a subject as rational that she can reason sufficiently well to count as having the power of reason; her beliefs and acts must at least sometimes be

---

[60] Any piece of hardware can be rendered unable to do something that it has the nomological capacity to do without destroying that capacity. An automobile can be rendered transiently unable to transport things from one location to another by a wire coming loose in the starter; but it would be incorrect to characterize it as having *lost* the nomological capacity to transport persons and property from one location to another.

[61] Psychologists have sometimes challenged the claim we are rational. See, e.g., Daniel Kahneman and Amos Tversky, "The Framing of Decisions and the Psychology of Choice," *Science,* vol. 211, no. 4481 (1981), 453–458. See also Daniel Kahneman, *Thinking Fast and Slow* (Farrar, Straus and Giroux, 2011), app. B.

conditioned by her reasoning.[62] Rationality is determined as much by what a subject believes and does as it is by how well she can reason about what should be believed and done. Accordingly, the two must be connected in the right way to warrant an attribution of rationality.

Practical rationality also requires a felt ability to distinguish among states of affairs in terms of how desirable they are and therefore in terms of their comparative value. While epistemic rationality requires being able to value true over false beliefs, practical rationality requires being able to rank states of affairs, at least roughly, according to their desirability. P counts as practically rational only if she is generally motivated to alter her behavior when needed to actualize a desired state or to avoid an undesired state and can hence be rationally induced to do so by content bearing on the occurrence of those states. And that requires the ability to rank them, at least roughly, by value.

To count as practically rational, one's decisions about what to do must be motivated by valuations grounded in the ability to experience some states of affairs as desirable and others as undesirable.[63] What distinguishes a valuation from a mere replica, facsimile, or simulation is that it is felt. It is true that a capacity on the part of P to predict the value-responses of other people can ground a valuation if P experiences their responses as having value that can rationally induce P to act in a manner likely to produce them. However, to count as *practically rational*, P must care enough about some value that it occasionally induces her to act as a means of realizing that value. Otherwise, she can do no more than mimic the psychological states and processes of beings who do count as such. The concept of practical rationality has to do with how people *decide* what they *do* – and hence with the connection between their ability to reason and their actions.

The claim that P is practically rational entails, then, that there is some state of affairs she cares enough about to try to actualize with her behavior. Norms of practical reasoning are concerned to ensure that the acts of rational self-interested subjects conduce to bringing about states of affairs that they generally desire to bring about because they should desire to bring about those states. Satisfaction of these norms thus conduces to bringing about the desired states by ensuring the agent's decisions are sound in the same way that satisfaction of the

---

[62] This should not be thought to require free will, as it is not clear we have free will in any robust sense. If we do not have free will, then our reasoning conditions our beliefs and acts only in the weak sense that the series of neurological states corresponding to steps in our reasoning causally produce the neurological states corresponding to the beliefs and acts they cause. It is because this claim is uncontentious, after all, that it is hard to grasp how our acts could be free in the sense metaphysical libertarianism claims we are.

[63] This entails that only beings who have some kind of agency *or* justifiably believe they do – as would be true of us even if systematically deceived by a Cartesian demon – count as practically rational; however, our conceptual practices pertaining to authority assume we are not systematically deceived by Cartesian demons. And it is those practices this Element seeks to theorize.

standards of logic conduces to believing only what is true by ensuring her reasoning is valid.[64]

There are, as was discussed in Section 8, three sources of value and thus of practical reasons – aesthetic, moral, and prudential. However, only one is relevant in explaining the conceptual normativity of authoritative tellings: since it is possible for authoritative tellings to require acts that are morally wicked and acts that are aesthetically undesirable (assuming this peculiar notion applies to ordinary acts), the only considerations that could explain the conceptual normativity of authoritative guidance are *prudential* in character.

What explains the prudential normativity of authoritative tellings, according to the Sanctions Thesis, is that they are backed by detriment reasonably contrived to deter enough noncompliance to enable the authority to minimally achieve the ends she intends to achieve by telling others what to do. The Sanctions Thesis requires no more by way of a developed capacity for discerning and weighing practical reasons than an ability to discern that a threat of detriment should be avoided, as a matter of prudential reasoning, and a disposition to avoid such detriment when possible in a manner that is minimally responsive to objective norms of *prudential* reasoning.

The idea that only the capacity to evaluate prudential considerations is relevant with respect to explicating the nature of practical authority uniquely coheres with this fact about us: while some of us are amoral, sociopathic, or worse, all of us are self-interested. If many of us are indifferent, and even hostile, to the demands of morality, no human being (or, for that matter, sentient nonhuman animal) is – or could be – indifferent to her own prudential interests.[65] We might not always do what we believe maximally conduces to our interests or get the prudential calculus right. But all of us care enough about our prudential interests that we want to avoid significant detriment when possible.

Even so, the claim that someone cares about her prudential interests does not entail that she is prudentially *rational*. Concern for one's interests is necessary, but not sufficient, to count as prudentially rational; one must also be epistemically rational as to one's beliefs about what does, and does not, conduce to one's prudential interests. A person who inflicts significant harm on herself on the strength of a delusion – which counts as such in virtue of being patently inconsistent with all

---

[64] What someone should desire can sometimes depend on what she antecedently desires. Although there are arguably things all rationally competent self-interested subjects should desire, there are also things that only rationally competent self-interested subjects with certain preferences should desire. If I want to get to Zagreb as quickly as possible, I should also want to take the first available flight.

[65] Approximately four percent of us – a chillingly high percentage – count as sociopathic in virtue of lacking a sense of self-restraint grounded in an ability to empathize with the feelings of other people. For a fascinating discussion of sociopathy and its prevalence in the population, see Martha Stout, *The Sociopath Next Door* (Harmony Books, 2005).

the available evidence – that it conduces to her well-being is not behaving in a manner that is prudentially rational.

The line between what counts as prudentially rational and what does not is difficult to draw because self-interested beings often take unjustified risks to realize trivial benefits; but this much is clear. Our conceptual practices assume that there is a line to be drawn here. They assume, in particular, that prudential rationality involves (i) a capacity to form beliefs about what conduces to one's prudential interests in a manner that is minimally responsive to objective standards of *epistemic* reasoning *and* (ii) a capacity to assess those beliefs in a manner that is minimally responsive to objective standards of *practical* reasoning.

A threat of detriment has two features that equip it to make a difference with respect to what rationally competent self-interested beings like us decide to do. First, it appeals to an interest shared of psychological necessity by all human beings (and sentient nonhuman animals) – namely, that in avoiding unpleasantness. One need be neither epistemically nor practically rational to have and act on this prudential interest. Newborn infants and sentient nonhuman animals instinctively – and immediately – exhibit aversive behaviors in response to painful stimuli. But while self-interested, they lack the developed capacities needed to count as rational.

Second, the use of threats to enforce authoritative tellings appeals to the most basic of our rational capacities. If the Sanctions Thesis is true, it is enough to constitute someone as able to stand in the authority relation that she can ascertain it is a bad idea, all else being equal, to resist an armed robber's demands and is presumptively motivated to comply for that reason. Rational competence, then, requires no more than just the ability to link some piece of detriment to noncompliance and an abiding disposition to avoid such detriment – that is, to accept and act on the view, to put the matter in Hulk-speak, "pain, bad."

The only plausible explanation of why the constitutive mechanisms of authoritative guidance are equipped to do what they are standardly used and needed to do among beings like us is that every telling that counts as authoritative is backed by detriment constituting a sanction: the only considerations rational self-interested beings like us can universally be presumed to value are those implicated by the Sanctions Thesis. There is just nothing else in these mechanisms that is remotely equipped to rationally induce potentially recalcitrant self-interested subjects like us to comply.

11 Practical Authority as the Power of Will-Imposition

Practical authority is partly constituted by a *power* to induce compliance. Someone lacking the right kind of power to induce members of a group to do as she directs lacks the requisite resources to guide their behavior by telling them what to do and, partly for this reason, does not count as having practical authority over them. Having the right kind of power to induce compliance in other people is foundational in equipping authority to perform its conceptual function of telling subjects what they must do.

To have a *power* to bring about a state of affairs $\underline{S}$ is to have the ability to bring it about that $\underline{S}$ occurs; it is incoherent to say P has a *power* to bring about something that she has no ability to bring about. *Dictionary.com* defines the term *power* as meaning "[the] *ability* to do or act," whereas *Merriam-Webster* defines it as meaning "[the] *ability* to act or produce an effect."[66]

The idea that P has a power to bring about some state of affairs $\underline{S}$ by doing $\underline{s}$ entails that P is minimally efficacious in bringing it about that $\underline{S}$ obtains by doing $\underline{s}$ when she does $\underline{s}$. This does not imply that she is trying to bring $\underline{S}$ about every time she does $\underline{s}$. But it does imply that when P does $\underline{s}$ to bring about $\underline{S}$, she succeeds often enough to minimally achieve the ends she seeks to achieve by doing $\underline{s}$. The claim that practical authority is constituted by a power to induce compliance implies that it is sufficiently efficacious in inducing compliance to enable the authority to minimally achieve her ends.

This power is not mechanistic. Whatever power an authority might have to induce compliance, it does not involve an ability to mechanistically cause subjects to do what she directs. It should be clear, for instance, that using a microchip implanted in someone's brain to mechanistically control what that person's body does by uttering imperative sentences does not count as exercising authority; one's imperatives in this instance are analogous to commands one might input into a computing device to cause it to perform some operation.

Our conceptual and nonconceptual practices presuppose that authoritative guidance is equipped, by nature, with the necessary resources to make a practical difference in what subjects decide to do, not by mechanistically causing a conforming act, but by inducing one. Though it might seem plausible to describe P mechanistically causing Q to do $\underline{s}$ as *inducing Q to do $\underline{s}$*, *causing Q to perform some action does not do so by making a practical difference in Q's decision-making because causal mechanisms circumvent Q's deliberative processes altogether.

Indeed, though it may seem plausible to describe Q in such instances as having been *induced* to do something, mechanistically causing her body to make the desired movements does not count as even *inducing Q to do something*, because such movements do not count as an *act*. Whatever it is that P may

[66] www.dictionary.com/browse/power; www.merriam-webster.com/dictionary/power (emphases added).

be seeking to achieve by causing Q's body to make the desired movements, it does not involve exercising practical authority over Q.

Practical authority can make a difference in a subject's deliberations about whether to comply only by *rationally inducing* her to comply – that is, by giving rise to something that she is likely to regard as a reason to comply because she should regard it as such.[67] Practical authority is thus constituted by a power to trigger preexisting reasons intended to rationally induce subjects to comply by *persuading* them to do so and is thus constituted by a power to persuade.

Theorists characterize practical authority's constitutive power to persuade using the less perspicuous – though far more titillating – idea of will-imposition; as Joseph Raz puts this conceptual truism, a person counts as having practical authority over others only if she is "effective in imposing [her] will on many over whom [she] claims authority."[68] Practical authority's constitutive power to induce compliance thus implicates an ability to rationally induce a subject to alter her will when she is not initially inclined to do what the authority says to do; a person cannot count as "effective" in imposing her will over subjects without having a power to do that. Although talk of will-imposition adds little beyond some sexy obscurity to what might otherwise be clearer, it is standard in the literature.

It is worth noting here that part of what explains the obscurity attending the notion of will-imposition is that the meaning of the locution "impose one's will" cannot be directly derived from the meaning of its constituent terms. It should be clear that, whatever kind of conscious mental state is picked out by the term *will*, whether it is an intention, volition, or preference of some kind, a conscious mental state is not something that can be imposed by one person on another person.

One might think it helpful to consider the notion of will-opposition (i.e., something done against a person's will), given that will-imposition and will-opposition *both* implicate the power to induce others to change their wills. However, practical authority's constitutive power of will-imposition cannot be explained in terms of the idea it does something *against* the will of subjects with respect to what it tells them to do. If P tells Q to do something and Q complies out of fear P will punish her if she fails to comply, then P has done something that constitutes imposing her will on Q without having done something against Q's will.

While it is uncontentious that will-opposition involves force, it is not clear whether or not will-imposition also does because the term *impose* is ambiguous

---

[67] This, of course, harmonizes nicely with the claim that authoritative tellings necessarily give rise to reasons to comply and the claim that the authority relation holds only among rationally competent beings, which were discussed above in Sections 8 and 10, respectively.

[68] Raz, *Ethics in the Public Domain*, 211.

between two uses. As *Merriam-Webster* defines these usages, *impose* means "to establish or bring about as if by force" and "to establish or apply by authority."[69] Although the former definition entails will-imposition involves force,[70] the latter definition does not: there is nothing in just our conventions for using *impose* that *transparently* entails practical authority can "establish or apply" something only by means that count as forceful.

The term *impose* might be ambiguous on the issue; but the idiomatic phrase *impose one's will* is not: as *Merriam-Webster* defines this phrase, it means "to force other people to do what one wants."[71] Given that our conceptual practices equate will-imposition with something that counts as force, practical authority's constitutive power of will-imposition can be explicated only in terms of a power involving the deployment of force as a means of rationally inducing compliance.

That said, we cannot reliably infer the Sanctions Thesis from the claim that practical authority is constituted by a power of will-imposition over subjects because the term *force* is also ambiguous. Though *force* is most commonly used to refer to a threat of violence as a means of inducing someone to do something that she does not want to do,[72] a second use is defined in terms of a power to persuade: *Oxford* defines this use as meaning a "[p]ower to convince or persuade the reason or judgement,"[73] while *Merriam-Webster* defines it as meaning a "capacity to persuade or convince."[74]

Our conceptual practices regarding epistemic authority differ from those regarding practical authority in one respect especially salient here: although it is a necessary condition for P to count as having practical authority over Q that P has the ability to do something reasonably contrived to persuade Q to do what P tells Q to do, it is *not* a necessary condition for P to count as having epistemic authority over Q that P has the ability to do something reasonably contrived to persuade Q to believe what P says should be believed.

Epistemic authority on some topic is wholly constituted by recognized expertise on it. An oncologist counts as an epistemic authority on cancer solely in virtue of her expertise – which is conferred by her education and acknowledged by her medical license. It is, after all, her expertise that explains why her diagnostic claims give rise to epistemic reasons to believe them. An oncologist

---

[69] www.merriam-webster.com/dictionary/impose.

[70] One might worry about the omission of *as if,* but it is not clear what counts as done *as if* by force. Although threatening force can induce someone to do something, bringing about something by threatening force does not amount to bringing it about *as if* by force.

[71] www.merriam-webster.com/dictionary/impose%20one%27s%20will.

[72] *Oxford* defines this usage as "coercion or compulsion, especially with the use or threat of violence." https://tinyurl.com/49hrhap9.

[73] www.oed.com/dictionary/force_n1?tab=meaning_and_use#4006739.

[74] www.merriam-webster.site/dictionary/force.

who is utterly unequipped to persuade patients of her claims and recommendations might be a shitty doctor, but she still counts as an epistemic authority on cancer. Expertise is enough to constitute someone as having epistemic authority because it is not a necessary condition for someone with expertise to have epistemic authority that she is efficacious in persuading others of her beliefs on the topic of her expertise.

Nevertheless, the claim is not that a person must *already* have the power to persuade subjects to do what they are told to count as having practical authority over them – beyond some basic ability to communicate content to others. The claim is that the norms conferring authority on a person do so by *endowing* her with the power to persuade by will-imposition.

That is, in part, what differentiates our conceptual practices pertaining to practical authority from those pertaining to other species of guidance. These norms confer authority on *P* by endowing *P* with a power to rationally induce a subject to comply when the subject is not initially inclined to do so. Since this equips *P* with the requisite power of persuasion, it follows that practical authority, unlike epistemic authority, is constituted by a power to persuade – in this instance, by the power to persuade subjects to do as they are told.

But practical authority differs from epistemic authority in terms of the mechanism it uses to persuade. When an epistemic authority desires to persuade, she does so by giving explanations that others are free to question. If an epistemic authority wants to persuade *Q* to believe/do something, then she will do so by explaining why it should be believed/done, on an evidentiary metric that *Q* regards, or should regard, as relevant. An oncologist counts as non-shitty at doctoring in virtue of being willing and able to explain her beliefs regarding a patient's condition in an accessible way that answers any questions the patient may have.

In contrast, a police officer who pulls you over on some highway need not attempt to convince you she is justified in pulling you over or ordering you to exit your car – though she should do both of these things (especially during these times of unrest between police and public). If a police officer finds it disrespectful to be questioned, she will respond by threatening arrest if you do not comply. But if she nonetheless answers your questions, she is likely to regard herself as having done you a favor. Although practical authority is partly constituted by the power to induce compliance by means of persuasion, people with practical authority, unlike those with epistemic authority, are, much more often than not, unwilling to explain themselves to subjects because they expect subjects to do what they are told when they are told. Indeed, this is part of what authoritative guidance is used to do – that is, to preempt debate.

It is true, of course, that practical authority must be able to create epistemic reasons for subjects to believe they should do what the authority tells them to do, but one need not be an epistemic authority to create epistemic reasons to believe what one says. It is enough, with respect to the majority of what we say, that we are regarded as credible and reasonably conscientious about verifying claims before making them. If Q knows that P carefully reads the newspaper and is honest about reporting what she reads, Q has a defeasible epistemic reason to believe what P says when P claims the paper said something. It suffices, then, to endow a practical authority P with the power to produce the applicable epistemic reasons, that Q justifiably believes that (i) a normative system $\underline{N}$ that antecedently governs her behavior confers practical authority on P to tell Q what to do with respect to acts over which $\underline{N}$ has jurisdiction *and* (ii) P is sincere when she tells Q to do something within that range of acts.

This power to persuade is what is picked out by the idea that practical authority is, by nature, effective in imposing its will on subjects. Someone who is equipped to persuade others to do $\underline{s}$ *only* by resorting to the devices used by epistemic authorities when they want to explain themselves does not count as having practical authority with respect to $\underline{s}$ because someone can count as having practical authority without being remotely inclined to explain herself. Persuasion by explanation has nothing to do with will-imposition or with the nature of practical authority. Practical authority's constitutive power of persuasion, then, must be explained by its constitutive power of will-imposition.

It is straightforward to show that the Sanctions Thesis explains practical authority's power of will-imposition. Since (1) the meaning of the locution "impose one's will" is "to *force* other people to do what one wants" and (2) the Sanctions Thesis explains authority's constitutive power to *persuade* in terms of a norm-governed capacity to en*force* its tellings, the Sanctions Thesis explains authority's constitutive power of will-imposition in terms of a power to persuade subjects to do as they are told as a means of avoiding the application of force.

It is even easier to show that *only* the Sanctions Thesis explains practical authority's constitutive power of will-imposition. While one might believe that there is nothing else in the practices constituting practical authority that explains this power, the argument is more direct: any measure that is reasonably contrived to "*force* other people to do what one wants" constitutes an en*force*ment device in virtue of being reasonably contrived to deter noncompliance. Given that the only way to *force* someone to perform an act that does not involve compulsion is by means that count as coercive, we can conclude that the Sanctions Thesis uniquely explains authority's constitutive power of will-imposition.[75]

---

[75] The application conditions of the relevant usage of *force* are as broad as those of *coerce*. As *Oxford* defines it, *force* is "coercion or compulsion, especially with the use or threat of violence." https://tinyurl.com/49hrhap9. The occurrence of *especially* in the definition assumes a person can threaten force without threatening violence: if P threatens to disclose embarrassing facts

The Sanctions Thesis incorporates both uses of *force* discussed above by explaining practical authority's constitutive power of will-imposition in terms of its norm-governed capacity to manufacture *normative* force by threatening *coercive* force: that we converge in believing we have an objective reason to avoid coercive force is what explains the ability of both coercion and force to make a practical difference in a subject's decision-making. Practical authority's constitutive power of will-imposition can be explained, then, only in terms of an ability to persuade by means that count as coercive and is thus *force*ful in both senses of the root term.[76]

It is worth noting that Raz's claim that an agent counts as having practical authority only if she is "effective in imposing [her] will on many over whom [she] claims authority" is inconsistent with his claim there can be law without sanctions in a society of angels. If, as I have argued here, practical authority's power of will-imposition must be explained by a norm-governed capacity to impose detriment for noncompliance, then Raz's society-of-angels argument is unsound. The problem is that there is no one with the requisite power of will-imposition in such a society because there is no one authorized to impose sanctions for noncompliance. Sanctions may not be needed to guide the behavior of angels, but they are needed to constitute a normative system as one of authority and thus as one of law.[77]

12 Practical Authority as Grounded in a Claim of Right

Practical authority is grounded in a claim of right – or, as it is sometimes described, a claim of authority.[78] What distinguishes the tellings of someone with a power to direct behavior in virtue of having practical authority from those of someone with just a power to do so is that the former are made under a claim of right that counts as plausible on some appropriate metric whereas the latter are not.

12.1 The Concept of a Claim

The term *claim* has a number of easily conflated usages. It is often used as a verb to suggest a nontrivial probability that a statement is either false or unjustified. As *Oxford* defines it, *claim* means "state or assert that something is the case, typically without providing evidence or proof."[79] This use of *claim* does not

---

about Q if she refuses to do s and Q does s to prevent their disclosure, then Q counts as having been forced *and* coerced to do s.

[76] This is why authoritative guidance, by its very nature, implicates a need for moral justification.

[77] I will say more about the society-of-angels argument in Section 15.

[78] If these two claims are distinct, the claim of *right* is the more basic one: it is the claim of right that someone has to direct behavior that grounds her claim of authority.

[79] https://tinyurl.com/4wv8333t.

assert that a piece of content is false or unjustified. But a word that expresses that some piece of content is asserted without evidence or proof can aptly be used to express skepticism about that content; a familiar example is "so you claim" when uttered in response to content one believes is dubious as a means of expressing that one believes it is dubious.

Something akin to this usage is often used in theorizing about the nature of law and authority: two famous examples are Joseph Raz's view that law claims legitimate authority and Robert Alexy's view that law claims moral correctness.[80] In both cases, the term *claim* is used as a verb to attribute an unsupported assertion to a legal system or – more plausibly, since normative systems are abstract objects incapable of agency[81] – to its officials. Given that judges often enforce morally problematic norms, an appropriate response to either such claim, without under-standing more about the salient qualities of the system and its norms, is the kind of skepticism insinuated by this verb-usage of *claim*.

But this is not the usage of interest; the relevant use of *claim* is as a noun that refers to a right that some person has or is believed to have. *Merriam-Webster* treats this usage as synonymous with one usage of the term *right*, defining it as "a right to something."[82] In contrast, *Collins* and *Dictionary.com* define it in terms of an appeal for something that is *believed* to fall within the scope of an entitlement; the former defines it as a "demand for something *you think* you have a right to," and the latter defines it as "a demand for something as due; an assertion of a right or an alleged right."[83]

The noun usage incorporates one feature of the verb usage relevant here – namely, that the content of the claim can be challenged – but it does not incorporate the insinuation that the content is false or lacking justification. Since practical authority must be conferred by a system of norms that otherwise governs the behavior of subjects, the claim of right is grounded in those norms, which constitute evidence of its veracity. The noun-usage signals that the content of the claim *could* be false without insinuating that it *is* false or lacking in needed evidence.

12.2 The Concept of a Right

The lexical meaning of the relevant usage of *right* is notoriously difficult to clarify because the term is defined in terms of synonyms that are as much in

---

[80] Raz, *Ethics in the Public Domain*, 215; Robert Alexy, "Law and Correctness," *Current Legal Problems*, vol. 51, no. 1 (1998), 205–221. For a criticism of Raz's view that applies to Alexy's, see Kenneth Einar Himma, *Morality and the Nature of Law* (Oxford University Press, 2019), ch. 5.

[81] See Himma, *Morality and the Nature of Law*, ch. 5.

[82] www.merriam-webster.com/dictionary/claim.

[83] www.collinsdictionary.com/dictionary/english/claim; www.dictionary.com/browse/claim. (italicized emphasis added).

need of clarification: *Collins* defines the term as meaning "what you are morally or legally *entitled* to do or to have," and *Merriam-Webster* defines it as "something to which one has a just claim: such as . . . the power or privilege to which one is justly *entitled*."[84]

These definitions are not especially helpful, but there is no need for an explication of the nature of a right because its most salient property for my purposes is clear.[85] To say that P has a right to do s̲ that is held against Q is to say, in part, that Q owes an obligation not to interfere with P's doing s̲: my constitutional speech right against the state defines a legal obligation on the part of officials not to interfere with my speech unless it is necessary to achieve a compelling state interest; my moral right to life defines a moral obligation on the part of others not to interfere with my continuing to live unless it is necessary to prevent me from culpably causing death or grievous bodily harm to others; and so on.

The right constituting P as having authority must thus be understood as defining an obligation not to interfere in ways deemed illicit with P's efforts to direct behavior that fall within its scope. While the complete range of what counts as illicit is not always clear, this much is: to the extent P is authorized to do something s̲ in directing the behavior of subjects that is otherwise impermissible under the relevant norms, P's right to do s̲ is constituted by an obligation on the part of her subjects not to interfere with her doing s̲ in ways that would otherwise be permissible under those norms.

12.3 The Concept of a Claim of Right

The meaning of the locution *claim of right* is straightforwardly derived from the meanings of its constituent terms. Given that (1) *claim* refers to an expressed view about the content of what is described as a *claim* and that (2) *right* refers to an obligation of noninterference on the part of those persons against whom the right is held, the locution *claim of right* refers to an expressed view about an obligation of noninterference owed by those against whom the right is held or thought to be held.

What this obligation requires is not clear. One might think it requires compliance, but this is false: Q does not do something that constitutes interfering with the exercise of P's authority simply by not complying. To *interfere* in a situation, as *Cambridge* defines it, is to "spoil[] it or prevent[] its progress."[86] If Q does not do what P tells her to do, then Q has violated an obligation if P has

---

[84] www.collinsdictionary.com/dictionary/english/right; www.merriam-webster.com/dictionary/right (italicized emphases added).
[85] See, e.g., Judith Jarvis Thomson, *The Realm of Rights* (Harvard University Press, 1990).
[86] https://dictionary.cambridge.org/us/dictionary/english/interfere.

authority to tell Q to do it. However, Q has not done anything that prevented P from telling her what to do.

Although Q is obligated to do what P tells her to do if P has practical authority over her, that does not follow from the claim Q has an obligation of noninterference; nonparties to the authority relation can also have such an obligation under the same norms conferring authority on P over Q but have no obligation to comply because they are not subject to P's authority: every soldier has a legal obligation to obey the orders of her commanding officer; but civilians also have a legal obligation not to interfere with the efforts of a commanding officer to direct the acts of soldiers under her authority.

The claim of right purports to justify tellings made under it by reference to the same norms conferring authority. The proposition that P does $\underline{s}$ under a claim of right expresses that P claims, expressly or impliedly, to be justified in doing $\underline{s}$ in virtue of having a right to do it and thus that P's doing $\underline{s}$ would otherwise be problematic. The notion that $\underline{s}$ is done under a *claim* of right implicitly acknowledges that a right is needed because $\underline{s}$ is otherwise prohibited under the same norms giving rise to the justifying claim of right.[87]

The claim that P has a *right* – as opposed to a *claim of right* – to do $\underline{s}$ under a system does not entail that doing $\underline{s}$ is otherwise prohibited by the system: the claim P has a legal right to speak her mind does not imply, for instance, it would otherwise be legally impermissible to do so; a legal system can permit something without conferring a right to do it by just not prohibiting it. The *claim of* language in the phrase *claim of right* implies or insinuates that a permission is needed to do what is done under claim of right because doing it is otherwise prohibited.

This permission defines the scope of the relevant obligation of noninterference. The claim that P has a permission under some set $\underline{N}$ of norms to do what others are not permitted to do under $\underline{N}$ entails that others have an obligation under $\underline{N}$ not to interfere with P's doing it in ways that would otherwise be allowed if $\underline{N}$ did not confer a permission on P to do it. A police officer has a legal permission to coercively detain an intoxicated driver that obligates others not to interfere in ways that would otherwise be permissible under the law.

The idea that it is a conceptual truth that law claims *moral* correctness or legitimacy, as Alexy and Raz believe, is thus rooted in a confusion about what

---

[87] A norm authorizing a judge to decide a case justifies her in deciding that case – that is, justifies her in asserting jurisdiction over the case. It does *not* necessarily justify the *content* of her decision under the relevant legal norms. One can challenge the content of a decision without challenging the judge's authority to decide the case. While there can be cases so badly decided that one can argue the judge lacked authority to decide them that way, these cases are comparatively unusual.

kinds of right can ground practical authority. Since practical authority need not be grounded in a moral right to direct behavior, there is absolutely nothing in the practices constituting a personal being as having practical authority that entails a claim of moral correctness or legitimacy. If, by nature, the law makes claims about its authority, those claims say nothing about law's moral qualities, because nothing in our conceptual practices entails that only morally justified tellings count as legally authoritative. Although there are usages of these terms concerned only with ideal systems of authoritative guidance and law, such usages are not relevant for my purposes.[88]

12.4 What Is a Plausible Claim of Right?

A claim of right must count as *plausible* to constitute someone as having practical authority over members of some group. A robber with a hyperactive sense of entitlement might claim she has a right to your money; however, that cannot even partly constitute her demand as authoritative because her claim is patently false and therefore obviously implausible. Even if she is a member of an organized criminal gang governed by norms requiring its members to rob nonmembers, those norms do not count as authoritative towards nonmembers.

To say that a claim is plausible is to say it should be believed, at least provisionally, in virtue of seeming likely to be true: *Collins* defines *plausible* as "*seem[ing]* likely to be true or valid," whereas *Merriam-Webster* defines the term as "*appearing* worthy of belief."[89]

The dictionary definitions identify a number of ways in which content might appear veridical but one is of fundamental importance. Content appears probable, reasonable, or worthy of belief only insofar as it appears likely to be true in light of the available evidence. To say a claim is plausible is therefore to make a defeasible prereflective judgment about its probable truth value – namely, that it is likely to be true. Since we are justified, at least provisionally, in believing what appears likely to be true, the characterization of a claim as *plausible* entails that subjects are *presumptively* justified in believing it without reflection on the strength of the evidence.

Whether a claim counts as plausible can vary from one group to another, depending on what evidence they have. Two thousand years ago, the claim the earth is flat counted as plausible simply in virtue of appearing flat in all directions because we had no evidence to the contrary: someone believing the earth is flat on the strength of those appearances was presumptively justified in

---

[88] For a discussion of an evaluative use of the term *law* that applies to an evaluative use of the term *authority*, see Himma, *Morality and the Nature of Law*, ch. 2.

[89] www.collinsdictionary.com/dictionary/english/plausiblee; www.merriam-webster.com/diction ary/plausible (italicized emphases added).

believing it, as would be a child with nothing more to go on than what her eyes tell her. But viewed against the background of what has been conclusively established by, among other things, photographs of the earth taken from space, the claim the earth is flat might *seem* plausible to someone who is unfamiliar with the overwhelming evidence. However, it *is* not plausible – that is, does not count as plausible.

The applicable standards of plausibility are hence socially constructed because they are determined by what we converge in believing is presumptively justified, as an objective matter, on the basis of the appearances. While these standards are ultimately conventional, we believe that they mirror objective standards that determine what counts, from a God's-eye perspective we cannot achieve, as *really* plausible. It is hence the doxastic reactions of those over whom someone claims authority that determine whether or not her claim counts as plausible.

Our conceptual practices pertaining to attributions of practical authority entail that two questions are especially pertinent in assessing the plausibility of *P*'s claim of right over members of a group: the first is whether there is a set of norms governing group members that confers a right upon *P* to direct their behavior; the second is whether members accept or acquiesce to *P*'s claim of right by complying enough when not initially inclined to do so to enable *P* to minimally achieve her ends.[90]

A claim of right counts as plausible as to members of a group, then, only if grounded in norms epistemically accessible to them. Although this does not entail subjects are aware of all the nuances of that claim, which would include details about its limits, it entails they are able to ascertain, without unreasonable difficulty, that someone claims a right to direct their behavior that is grounded in those norms – whether because those norms are published in a medium to which subjects have easy access or whether because they are easily deduced from either the behavior of persons claiming such a right or the behavior of others subject to this claim.

Note that *Q*'s acquiescing to a claim of right plays the same role in determining its plausibility that *Q*'s contracting with another person plays in determining the plausibility of the claim that *Q* is contractually obligated to that person. Inasmuch as whether we agree to a contractual obligation determines the *truth* of claims pertaining to whether we are contractually obligated, it determines the *plausibility* of these claims. If my agreeing to a set of contractual obligations constitutes the claim I have these obligations as true, then it also constitutes that claim as plausible to me, since the fact I agreed to them is epistemically

---

[90] See Section 6.

accessible to me. If a person understands all the relevant facts constituting a claim as true and understands these facts constitute that claim as true, then she knows all she needs to know in order to discern the appearance of its likely truth and thus its plausibility.

Acquiescing to the requisite claim of right constitutes it as plausible in the following way. Since Q's acquiescing to P's claim is partly constituted by a disposition to comply, it involves treating P's claim as true and thus as plausible. Insofar as Q is aware P claims the same right over others who acquiesce and thereby manifest a similar disposition to comply, Q's awareness of these facts constitutes P's claim of right over *them* as plausible to Q. But if everyone else who accepts or acquiesces to P's claim is aware that others over whom P claims authority also accept or acquiesce to it, thereby manifesting a similar disposition to comply, then P's claim of right counts as plausible to all group members.

The plausibility of authority's constitutive claim of right is, then, determined by the following social facts: (1) the claim of right is grounded in public norms that are knowable (and usually understood in broad outlines) by members of the relevant group; (2) members converge in accepting or acquiescing to it, thereby manifesting a disposition to comply that enables the authority to minimally achieve the ends she wishes to achieve by directing their behavior; and (3) each member is aware that all the others accept or acquiesce to it, thereby manifesting the conceptually requisite disposition that enables the authority to minimally achieve her ends.

It bears reiterating that norms confer practical authority by creating a permission to do what is otherwise prohibited – by authorizing a person to do it. Legal norms authorize judges in criminal cases to order bailiffs to remove the defendant from the courtroom and transport her to another place where she will be incarcerated, thereby creating a permission to do so. Absent that permission, ordering a person to be taken and transported from one place and incarcerated in another would constitute, in every existing legal system, criminal intent to kidnap her.

Creation of a special permission to direct behavior in the form of a right to do so is the only mechanism by which a system can confer something that counts, on our conceptual practices, as practical authority: a system $\underline{N}$ of norms counts as conferring authority on P to do something that counts as directing the behavior of others within its jurisdiction only if $\underline{N}$ prohibits subjects from doing that something but authorizes and thereby entitles P to do it.

12.5 Practical Authority's Constitutive Claim of Right and the Sanctions Thesis

The Sanctions Thesis uniquely explains this constitutive feature of practical authority: the only explanation of the notion that authority must be exercised under a plausible claim of right that presumptively justifies it is that a telling can count as authoritative only if backed by detriment. It is because a judge is legally authorized to enforce her tellings by imposing detriment in the form of a fine or incarceration that her tellings must be grounded in a claim of *legal* right that *legally* justifies doing so; she needs a *legal* right to do so because the law does not permit others to fine or sentence people to incarceration. That a judge is authorized by *legal* norms to do what is otherwise unlawful explains why her tellings count as *legally* authoritative only if made under a plausible claim of *legal* right, which justifies her, at least presumptively, under the *law* in issuing those tellings.[91]

There is simply nothing else in the practices constituting authoritative guidance that needs a justification *of any kind* – including moral justification. Practical authority guides behavior through utterances that tell the subject what to do. However, uttering a sentence purporting to tell someone what to do no more needs to be done under claim of right than uttering any other sentence does: I am as much permitted to say "you must do this" as I am to say "the sky is blue" under any system of norms governing my behavior I know of, other than those of etiquette. It is the fact that the authority's utterances telling people what to do are permissibly enforced by detriment severe enough to deter noncompliance that explains why authoritative tellings need a justification.

It might be helpful to note how the claim that practical authority is partly constituted by a plausible claim of right is explained by the claim that it is partly constituted by a power of will-imposition. It is not surprising that rationally competent self-interested beings like us sometimes resist being told what to do, given that authority's capacity to tell others what to do must be explained in terms of a permission to do what others are not permitted to do. Because an authoritative telling comes bundled with a claim that the teller has a right to do something others are not permitted to do, it can offend the subject's sense of autonomy and equality.[92] The fact that these power inequalities, like economic inequalities, sometimes elicit rebellious feelings in rational self-interested subjects like us in worlds like ours where we must compete for everything we need or want is not in the least surprising.

None of this tells us anything about whether the practices conferring authority on someone to enforce her tellings in any particular society are morally justified, but that is a strength of the theory – and not a defect. Any conceptual theory of practical authority that entails that the claim of right must be morally justified is inconsistent with *our* conceptual practices and fails to explicate them for that

---

[91] It does not necessarily justify the content of the relevant tellings. See n. 87.

[92] It does not help in this regard that practical authorities and their subjects are sometimes invidiously – and ill-advisedly – described as *superiors* and *subordinates*.

reason; our conceptual practices assume there can be illegitimate – or morally unjustified – authority. The requisite justification is internal to the system conferring authority. Accordingly, it is the same norms that confer authority which function to justify enforcing authoritative tellings within that system of norms.

13 Practical Authority as Giving Rise to Obligations

One of the distinguishing features of practical authority is that its tellings create obligations to comply. If a judge tells me to do something within the scope of her *legal* authority to tell me to do, then it follows that I am *legally* obligated to do it; if my employer tells me to do something within the scope of her contractual authority to tell me to do, then it follows that I am contractually obligated to do it; and so on. The idea that a telling defines an obligation to comply is simply part of what we express when we describe it as *authoritative.*[93]

There are two constitutive properties of practical authority that distinguish it from power. The first, discussed above in Section 12, is that authoritative tellings, unlike those of someone who has just power, are made under a claim of right that counts as plausible in virtue of being accepted or acquiesced to by those who are subject to the teller's authority. The second, discussed in this section, is that authoritative tellings, unlike those of someone with only a power, create obligations to comply *of the same type as the norms conferring authority on the teller.* As Hart famously points out, an armed robber's tellings can *oblige* compliance but cannot, unlike those of practical authority, obligate it.[94]

These two constitutive properties are related. Part of what explains why a practical authority's tellings give rise, by nature, to an obligation to comply is that they are grounded in a right *to direct behavior*; any set of norms conferring a right on P to direct Q's behavior does so partly in virtue of requiring

---

[93] The concept of obligation has gotten comparatively little attention in the literature. While Jeremy Bentham, John Austin, and H. L. A. Hart all had something to say about it, most contemporary theorists have focused on distinguishing one kind of obligation from another (e.g., legal from moral obligation) or explicating the nature of a particular kind of obligation (e.g., legal obligation). See, most recently, Stefan Bertea, *A Theory of Legal Obligation* (Cambridge University Press, 2019); Dan Wodak, "What Does 'Legal Obligation' Mean?" *Pacific Philosophical Quarterly*, vol. 99, no. 4 (2018), 790–816.

[94] Following H. L. A. Hart, I use the term *oblige* to refer to a particular kind of prudential response to a choice situation; as Hart describes the usage, "The gunman orders his victim to hand over his purse and threatens to shoot him if he refuses; if the victim complies we refer to the way in which he was <u>forced</u> to do so by saying he was *obliged* to do so. To some it has seemed clear that in this situation where one person gives another an order backed by threats, and <u>in this sense of 'oblige,'</u> we have the essence of law, or at least 'the key to the science of jurisprudence.'" Hart, *The Concept of Law*, 3rd ed. (Clarendon Press, 2012), 6 (underlined emphasis added). Although Hart appears to limit this usage only to contexts involving threats of physical or emotional coercion, I use the term to include responses to contexts in which a significant benefit is promised. On this broader use, one counts as obliged to cash in a winning lottery ticket, instead of throwing it away and foregoing the cash prize.

that Q do what P tells her to do – that is, by creating an obligation that binds Q. It is true that any robust right to free speech permits P, absent unusual circumstances, to address a sentence r to Q that purports to tell Q to do something; however, the fact P uttered a telling in the exercise of her free speech rights cannot, by itself, obligate Q to do what that utterance says must be done. What creates Q's obligation to comply are the norms that confer authority on, and thereby authorize, P to direct Q's behavior; these norms confer a right on P to direct Q's behavior by obligating Q to do what P tells her to do.

As will be discussed below, obligations bind by creating liabilities to detriment that rational self-interested subjects like us prefer to avoid, all else being equal, as a descriptive matter of fact, because we should prefer to avoid it, all else being equal, as an objective matter of practical reasoning. Indeed, it is the fact that obligations create liabilities which explains how they give rise, as a matter of conceptual necessity, to objective reasons that motivate compliance and to objective reasons that justify it. The idea that obligations bind by creating liabilities is at the core of the relevant conceptual and nonconceptual practices.

13.1 Obligations as Binding

The content of *our* concept of obligation is determined by our conventions for using the term *obligation* together with the shared philosophical assumptions about its nature that condition and ground those semantic conventions. *Oxford* defines the term *obligation* as meaning "an act or course of action to which a person is morally or legally *bound*," whereas *Merriam-Webster* defines it as meaning "something one is *bound* to do."[95]

As the italicized language indicates, the claim that obligations *bind* is foundational to both our conceptual and nonconceptual practices regarding *obligation*. As Hart explains ordinary usage:

> The figure of a *bond* binding the person obligated, which is buried in the word "obligation," and the similar notion of a debt latent in the word "duty" are explicable in terms of . . . a chain binding those who have obligations so that they are not free to do what they want.[96]

These truisms comprise the foundation of our conceptual practices regarding the nature of obligation.

It is also true, though not as obvious, that the mechanism through which obligations bind cannot be explained just in terms of the subject's feeling unfree to do what she would otherwise feel free to do. As Hart observes:

---

[95] www.oed.com/dictionary/obligation_n?tab=meaning_and_use#34088866; www.merriam-webster.com/dictionary/obligation (emphases added).
[96] Hart, *The Concept of Law*, 87.

Natural and perhaps illuminating though these figures or metaphors are [i.e., that of a chain binding those with obligations], we must not allow them to trap us into a misleading conception of obligation as essentially consisting in some feeling of pressure or compulsion experienced by those who have obligations. The fact rules of obligation are generally supported by serious social pressure does not entail that to have an obligation under the rules is to experience feelings of compulsion or pressure.[97]

Whatever it is that explains how obligations bind, our conceptual practices assume that the mechanism is objective, and not subjective.

The problem is to identify this mechanism by which obligation does something that counts as binding subjects, on our conceptual practices. Section 13.2 explicates the nature of obligation in terms of its constitutive properties and argues that obligations *bind* by creating liabilities in the form of potential exposure to detriment that subjects prefer to avoid, all else being equal, as a descriptive matter of fact, because they should prefer to avoid it, all else being equal, as a matter of practical reasoning.[98] This section concludes that these liabilities explain how obligations bind in terms of the reasons to which they give rise as a matter of conceptual necessity.

13.2 The Constitutive Properties of Obligation

The constitutive properties of – that is,. the existence or application conditions for – obligation, as our conceptual practices construct that notion, can be roughly summarized as follows: P has an obligation to do s under N if and only if (1) N is a normative system; (2) there is a mandatory norm n in N that governs P's behavior; (3) n requires that P do s; (4) N excludes certain considerations as excusing or justifying noncompliance with n; (5) n binds P in virtue of implicating a liability subjects regard as detriment to be avoided, all else being equal, because they should regard it as such; (6) n creates an objective reason that justifies P in doing s under N and immunizes P in N against the imposition of the relevant liability; and (7) n creates an objective reason that should motivate, all else being equal, the agent to comply that is grounded in the undesirability of the liability to which N gives rise.[99]

---

[97] Ibid., 138.

[98] One might think obligations bind in part by creating second-order exclusionary reasons. but I will argue in Section 14 that objective exclusionary reasons do not exist. However, either way, it should be clear that obligations bind by creating liabilities that give rise to first-order reasons to comply grounded in the detriment constituting the liability. If obligations give rise to exclusionary reasons as a matter of conceptual necessity, those reasons must also be grounded in the detriment constituting the liability. There is simply nothing else in the constitutive properties of obligation that is equipped to do that normative work.

[99] Contrast with Stefan Bertea's view that "obligation is best conceived as a practically normative requirement that makes a perceptible and yet empirically resistible claim on us, who in turn do

13.3 Obligations Bind by Creating Liabilities

The only one of these claims needing explication for my purposes is the claim that obligations create liabilities as a matter of conceptual necessity; this is the only claim of the seven above that one might sensibly think does not obviously express a conceptual truism about the nature of obligation.[100]

Obligations bind by defining a consequence to which the subject is liable. While the term *liable* is most frequently used in connection with the law,[101] it can be used in connection with other species of prescription: as *Merriam-Webster* explains this usage, it means "being in a position to incur" and "subject to some usually adverse contingency or action."[102] It might feel more natural to limit the application of this term to the law, but the term is aptly applied, as a matter of ordinary usage, to other prescriptions, social and nonsocial alike.

One can count as *liable* only to detriment because one can *incur*, or be *subject to*, only detriment. As *Cambridge* defines it, *incur* means to "to experience something bad as a result of actions you have taken."[103] Given that it is inapt to describe winning a lottery as "something bad," it is inapt to describe someone who buys a ticket as "incurring" the prize money or as "liable" to winning it.

It is likewise inapt to characterize someone who buys a lottery ticket as being "subject to" the winnings. Though the prize money is correctly characterized as "subject to" taxation, this is because having one's winnings taxed counts as detriment constituting a tax liability. The term *liability* applies only to what members of the group regard as detriment in virtue of preferring to avoid it, all else being equal, because they should prefer to avoid it, all else being equal.

Our conceptual practices do *not* entail that detriment counts as a *liability* in a system only if it is reasonably likely to deter enough noncompliance to enable the system to minimally achieve its ends. It is clear, for instance, that the liabilities defined by mandatory moral norms are *not* sufficiently severe to deter enough

---

something presumptively wrong, for which we can be held accountable, insofar as we fail to abide by it," which he describes as "the fundamental, or essential, and so minimal characterization of obligation." Bertea, *A Theory of Legal Obligation*, ch. 1, sec. 4.

[100] One might think that moral obligations are a counterexample to the claim that obligations are constituted, by nature, by a liability, but this is false. Violating a moral obligation constitutes one as deserving of blame, censure, or punishment. Since we regard being *deserving* of blame, censure, or punishment as detriment we prefer to avoid, it counts as a liability – albeit one that lacks the teeth of *being* blamed, censured, or punished. Most of us care a great deal about the requirements of morality, though we might disagree on the content of those requirements. We want not just to be *regarded as* good but to actually *be* good.

[101] *Merriam-Webster* defines the narrower usage as "obligated according to law or equity" and "subject to appropriation and attachment." www.merriam-webster.com/dictionary/liable.

[102] www.merriam-webster.com/dictionary/liable. Though the *Merriam-Webster* definition states that the contingency is "*usually* adverse," one is inaptly described as either "in a position to incur" or "subject to" a contingency that is not adverse.

[103] https://dictionary.cambridge.org/us/dictionary/english/incur.

noncompliance to enable the system of morality to minimally achieve whatever ends are plausibly attributed to it.[104] If they were, then we would not need law's coercive strictures to enable us to live together in comparative peace. Assuming it is a necessary condition, as I argue in this Element, for a telling to count as authoritative that it is backed by detriment severe enough to enable the teller to minimally achieve her ends, no such requirement applies to the concept of a liability.

Understanding how the idea of liability figures into our conceptual and nonconceptual practices pertaining to obligation requires understanding a number of logical relationships that obtain among a cluster of concepts. Most conspicuously, obligation is related to wrongness in the following way: the claim that P has an obligation to do $\underline{a}$ is logically equivalent to – albeit not synonymous with – the claim that it is wrong for P to abstain from doing $\underline{a}$. The only way to do wrong, on our conceptual practices, is to violate an obligation.

The concept of wrongness is related to that of culpability, but the relationship is more complicated. One counts as culpable only if one does wrong in virtue of not having met an obligation, but one can do wrong without being culpable: if P is legally insane and provably commits a murder, then P has committed a *legal* wrong – despite the fact she lacks the abilities needed for *legal* culpability and is immunized from punishment for this reason. Moreover, it is plausible to think that one can count as culpable for an action that is not wrong: if P tells Q something, mistakenly believing it is false, and this is not intended as a joke, then P's uttering it to Q is correctly described as *culpable* – indeed, even if P's uttering it to Q does not count as wrong because it turns out to be true, contrary to what P believes. But, either way, it is clear both that the term *wrong* applies only to acts and that the term *culpable* applies only to mental states, like intentions.

The concepts of obligation, wrongness, and culpability are related to that of liability in the following ways: P counts as liable only for acts she is obligated not to perform; P counts as liable only for acts that count as wrong in virtue of violating some obligation; and P counts as liable only for acts that count as culpable. Someone can thus count as culpable only for acts that count as wrong.

One counts as liable to detriment in virtue of deserving it for having culpably done wrong under the same system of norms giving rise to the obligation. Moral norms defining obligations create a liability in the form of being subject to blame, censure, or punishment in virtue of deserving it under these norms. Social norms of etiquette defining obligations create a liability in the form of being subject to social disapproval in virtue of deserving it under those norms. Criminal laws defining obligations create a liability in the form of being subject to fines or incarceration in virtue of one's deserving it under the same norms.

---

[104] See n. 100.

This liability explains the normative force of the obligation and the reason to which it gives rise. Obligations bind by creating liabilities that subjects have objective motivating reasons to avoid. One cannot be immunized against the imposition of the detriment to which one is liable simply because one regards oneself, correctly or not, as having had conclusive conflicting reasons. If these reasons are excluded as excusing or justifying noncompliance, they cannot immunize one against the detriment that one deserves under the norms creating the obligation and corresponding liability. It is therefore the objective motivating reason to avoid the detriment one deserves for noncompliance that expresses the sense in which one *must* or *shall,* as opposed to merely *should*, do what the corresponding norm requires.

It is tempting to think prescriptions creating obligations have a normativity lacking in prescriptions that do not create obligations; however, that is a mistake. While we do not conceptualize nonobligatory mandatory prescriptions as defining liabilities, the two kinds of prescriptions *both* implicate detriment, albeit a little differently. Obligatory mandatory prescriptions do so by creating liabilities that are *justifiably* imposed under the same system that constitutes them as obligatory, whereas nonobligatory mandatory prescriptions do not define such liabilities, even if backed by detriment.[105]

Indeed, it is worth noting here that noncompliance with a nonobligatory mandatory prescription can result in the imposition of far more severe detriment than noncompliance with an obligatory mandatory prescription. Being shot in the face for disobeying a robber's telling is obviously less desirable, as an objective matter of practical reasoning, than being deserving of blame for culpably telling some innocuous lie. The conceptual normativity of obligatory mandatory prescriptions cannot be distinguished from that of other mandatory prescriptions in terms of the severity of the detriment backing them.

The only conceptual difference between the two kinds of prescription relevant here is that obligatory mandatory prescriptions create objective justifying reasons as a matter of conceptual necessity by giving rise to novel liabilities, whereas nonobligatory mandatory prescriptions do not. But this distinction does not correspond to any conceptual difference regarding normativity because justifying reasons do not count, strictly speaking, as reasons to comply since they operate to justify, rather than to rationally induce, compliance. That the law defines a justification for killing someone in self-defense does not, by itself, trigger an objective motivating reason to do so. It is the person's interest in continuing to live that gives rise to that reason to do so by triggering it.

---

[105] I assume, for the sake of argument, there can be prescriptions that count as mandatory despite not being backed by detriment to avoid begging any questions. But, as will be recalled, I argued in Section 7 that every prescription that counts as mandatory is backed by detriment.

13.4 The Concept of Obligation and the Sanctions Thesis

The claim that every telling that counts as authoritative is backed by *detriment* is entailed by the claims that (a) authoritative tellings define obligations and (b) obligations bind by creating liabilities. Since a person can be obligated to comply with a telling only if it creates a liability for noncompliance, it follows that every telling giving rise to an obligation creates a liability for noncompliance. Since, further, something counts as a liability only if it exposes subjects to detriment for noncompliance by placing them "in a position to incur" it, thereby constituting them as "subject to" it, a person counts as obligated under a system of norms only if that system puts her in a position to incur, thereby making her subject to, detriment for noncompliance.[106] But since a telling counts as authoritative only if it defines an obligation to comply, it follows that every telling that counts as authoritative is backed by something that counts as detriment.

The Sanctions Thesis expresses a stronger claim than just that every telling that counts as authoritative is backed by something that counts as detriment; it asserts, further, that every telling that counts as authoritative is backed by detriment sufficiently severe – and therefore reasonably likely – to deter enough noncompliance to enable the teller to minimally achieve those ends that she intends to achieve by directing the behavior of subjects. Since a telling can be backed by detriment insufficiently severe to do that work,[107] the Sanctions Thesis cannot be *deduced* from the claim that every telling that counts as authoritative creates a liability that constitutes an obligation to comply.

Nonetheless, it *can* justifiably be inferred as the best explanation of how authoritative tellings necessarily give rise to obligations to comply with the help of an uncontentious claim about the constitutive properties of authoritative tellings. If a telling counts as authoritative only if efficacious in deterring enough noncompliance among subjects to enable the teller to minimally achieve her ends, it is because the liability that constitutes the telling as binding is reasonably contrived, and therefore equipped, to deter enough noncompliance to enable her to minimally achieve those ends.

Further, one can infer the Sanctions Thesis with the help of a somewhat weaker claim about the constitutive efficacy of authoritative guidance – namely, that every telling that counts as authoritative is issued by someone efficacious in inducing compliance in subjects not already disposed to comply. This weaker claim does not imply every authoritative telling *succeeds* in deterring enough

---

[106] www.merriam-webster.com/dictionary/liable.

[107] Proponents of more stringent penalties for crime typically ground their views in claims that existing penalties are not sufficiently severe to reduce the incidence of crime to what they believe are acceptable levels.

noncompliance to enable the authority to minimally achieve her ends; that something is reasonably contrived to perform some function does not entail it is successful in performing it. But the only plausible explanation of why authoritative guidance is, by nature, minimally efficacious in guiding behavior is that only tellings that are reasonably contrived to deter enough noncompliance to enable the authority to minimally achieve her ends count as authoritative.

A telling that is not reasonably contrived to deter enough noncompliance to enable the authority to minimally achieve her ends by guiding the behavior of subjects is not reasonably contrived to do what authoritative tellings are standardly needed and used to do – namely, to induce compliance in subjects who are not already disposed to comply. If part of what constitutes an authoritative telling as reasonably contrived to perform this function is that it gives rise to an obligation as a matter of conceptual necessity, the liability constituting an authoritative telling as binding – and, accordingly, as obligatory – must be reasonably contrived to deter enough noncompliance to enable the authority to minimally achieve her ends and counts as a sanction, as I have explicated that concept. Since there can be wicked authoritative tellings that neither give rise to novel moral obligations nor conform to preexisting ones, the Sanctions Thesis is the only plausible explanation of how authoritative tellings define obligations to comply as a matter of conceptual necessity.

14 Must Authoritative Tellings Create Exclusionary Reasons?

The Exclusionary Thesis asserts that mandatory prescriptions create exclusionary reasons which, by nature, bar subjects from acting on certain conflicting first-order reasons.[108] Since it is a truism that every telling counts as a mandatory prescription, the Exclusionary Thesis entails that every telling that counts as authoritative gives rise to a second-order exclusionary reason (i.e., that every authoritative telling necessarily triggers a second-order exclusionary reason).

Exclusionary reasons are objective and motivating in character. Since the only kind of reason that could function to bar an agent from acting on a motivating reason is another motivating reason, exclusionary reasons count as motivating reasons. Since, as Raz claims, one should treat mandatory prescriptions as exclusionary reasons,[109] they likewise count as objective. They also count, of course, as subjective for a subject if she treats them as having normative force in

---

[108] As Raz puts it, "mandatory norms are exclusionary reasons." Raz, *Practical Reason and Norms*, 72. To the extent authoritative tellings count as mandatory prescriptions, they also count as exclusionary reasons.

[109] Raz claims that rationally competent subjects "may be justified in not acting on the balance of [first-order] reasons." Ibid., 39.

her decision-making. However, they count as objective, on Raz's view, because the subject *should* regard these prescriptions as exclusionary reasons.

Raz discusses three deliberative conflict situations that he believes can be resolved by recourse to objective exclusionary reasons. However, it suffices to consider one because each has a similar structure and is thus adequately addressed with a similar analysis. Raz's example of Jeremy's reasoning in one of these situations is particularly germane since it is concerned with the nature of authority:

> Jeremy is ordered by his commanding officer to appropriate and use a van belonging to a certain tradesman. Therefore, he has a reason to appropriate the van. His friend urges him to disobey the order pointing to weighty reason for doing so. Jeremy does not deny that his friend may have a case. But, he claims, it does not matter whether he is right or not. Orders are orders and should be obeyed even if wrong, even if no harm will come from disobeying them. . . . The order is a reason for doing what you were ordered regardless of the balance of the reasons.[110]

As Raz represents Jeremy's thinking, the order precludes his acting on his own assessment of the order's moral character: "It means that it is not for you to decide what is best."[111]

Two observations would be helpful here. First, this is a thought experiment and not a report of some rigorous empirical study of our conceptual practices. In essence, Raz has simply written his views on how Jeremy should think on whether to comply into the example. But without rigorous social scientific empirical confirmation, these views are not justifiably attributed to ordinary speakers, whose convergent beliefs about what the norms of practical reasoning require help to determine the content of our evaluative practices.[112] In consequence, these examples show nothing more momentous than that recourse to exclusionary reasons is objectively rational (i.e., that recourse to exclusionary reasons is *not objectively irrational*). Unfortunately, all this entails is that the Exclusionary Thesis is a coherent thesis about the nature of a mandatory prescription.[113]

Second, it is clear that Jeremy can justifiably reach the same result without recourse to second-order motivating exclusionary reasons if he conceptualizes orders as giving rise to first-order motivating reasons that can be outweighed only in exceptional cases, as when needed to prevent perpetuating a gross

---

[110] Ibid.   [111] Ibid.   [112] But see n. 22 and associated text.

[113] Given that it is a necessary condition for a subject to count as rational, as was seen in Section 10, that her reasoning minimally conforms to what we take to be objective standards of epistemic and practical reasoning, the relevant notions of coherence and rationality track each other in the following way: A subject's reasoning counts as rational if and only if it is coherent. Accordingly, a subject's reasoning counts as irrational if and only if it is incoherent. The idea of coherence assumes that the subject's thinking about whether to perform some act is connected in the right way with whether it should be performed. Rationality, again, defines a comparatively low bar.

injustice. This conforms to our shared views about the nature of orders: not even the United States Code of Military Justice requires a soldier to obey every order.[114] Further, since the concept of an exclusionary reason was unfamiliar to philosophers until Raz invented it,[115] it is much more plausible to think ordinary speakers conceive orders as giving rise to only weighty first-order reasons to do what they require.

This latter point would not surprise Raz, as he takes pains to avoid overselling the Exclusionary Thesis; Raz never so much as insinuates that objective standards of practical reasoning ever *require* us to consider second-order exclusionary reasons. Indeed, on the first page of chapter 1 of *Practical Reasons and Norms*, Raz describes his goal as "to show that these distinctions are plausible and useful."[116] Although he claims that "a useful explication of the notions of strength, weight, and overriding . . . *must* allow for the existence of other logical types of conflict and of conflict resolution,"[117] he never gives any arguments in support of the claim that recourse to such reasons is even sometimes required. All the examples he discusses in the book are more easily – and naturally – resolved just by considering all of the first-order motivating reasons.

One might think this is enough to establish that first- and second-order mechanisms for resolving conflict are on the same level. But this overlooks that first-order mechanisms are indispensable in constituting mandatory prescriptions as defining wrongs. Without a mandatory moral norm to define an objective first-order motivating reason to abstain from, say, intentionally killing people, there is no problem *of any order* in doing so. There is no first-order problem because there is no moral norm to define a wrong and no second-order problem because there is no norm of any kind to cause the problem; without a mandatory moral norm to define a set of excluded reasons, there are no relevant objective exclusionary reasons. If objective exclusionary motivating reasons are needed to perform some function in our practical reasoning, it is, as Raz believes, to protect the relevant objective first-order motivating moral reasons by augmenting them.

But it is not clear why the objective first-order moral motivating reasons created by a mandatory moral prescription, as a matter of conceptual necessity, need such protection or why only objective exclusionary moral motivating reasons are equipped to protect them. The idea that mandatory moral prescriptions necessarily give rise to objective exclusionary moral motivating reasons might seem plausible inasmuch as we conceive moral obligations as giving rise to moral motivating reasons that trump prudential motivating reasons. But

---

[114] It requires only that "lawful orders" be obeyed. 10 U.S.C. 892; UCMJ art. 92.
[115] See Section 4.2.   [116] Raz, *Practical Reason and Norms*, 15.   [117] Ibid., 36.

a second-order exclusionary *moral* motivating reason is needed to neutralize countervailing first-order *prudential* motivating reasons only when those first-order reasons to perform some wrongful act *objectively* outweigh the first-order motivating moral reason to abstain from its performance.

The notion that prudential considerations *ever* defeat the objective first-order moral motivating reasons to which mandatory moral prescriptions give rise cannot be reconciled with our evaluative moral practices. Consider the moral norm that prohibits torture. If our ordinary evaluative practices define the touchstone, then the first-order moral reason not to torture a person necessarily outweighs any prudential benefits that may accrue to you from doing so. Even if someone promises you a trillion dollars to torture someone for just ten seconds, it is wrong to do so; the moral cost to human dignity vastly exceeds any prudential benefits to you. Accordingly, from the vantage point of shared views about what objective standards require of moral reasoning, the existence of objective second-order exclusionary reasons is otiose.

There is no work that objective exclusionary reasons are *needed* to do in explaining our conceptual practices pertaining to authoritative guidance. If it were true that only legitimate tellings count as authoritative, the objective first-order *moral* motivating reasons to comply would do all the needed work. Those reasons either outweigh the countervailing first-order motivating reasons or they do not. But if not, there is no ground for thinking that there must be an objective exclusionary moral reason that tips the balance in favor of compliance by excluding the conflicting first-order motivating reasons. Further, if the Sanctions Thesis is true, the objective first-order motivating reasons – which include moral motivating reasons if the authority is legitimate – do all the needed deliberative work. In neither case are there grounds to think objective standards of practical reasoning require recourse to exclusionary motivating reasons.

But the idea there is no work *objective* exclusionary motivating reasons are needed to do under norms of practical reasoning entails that these reasons do not exist. If a proposition counts as an objective reason only if it favors doing, or abstaining from doing, something under objective norms of practical reasoning, then a proposition that does no deliberative work under these norms (i.e. objectively favors nothing) does not count as an objective reason. However, if it does not count as an objective reason, then it does not exist as such. Although this does not preclude subjects from treating some proposition as giving rise to an exclusionary reason, it implies that any subject who does so, thinking it is an objective requirement of practical reasoning, has made a mistake.[118]

---

[118] The analysis is agnostic with respect to whether there are objective second-order exclusionary justifying reasons.

But, either way, assuming the Exclusionary Thesis is true, the objective exclusionary motivating reasons to which a mandatory prescription gives rise in virtue of its nature must express the same kind of value that is expressed by the first-order motivating reason to which it gives rise in virtue of its nature. It should be clear that (a) the only objective motivating reasons to which mandatory moral prescriptions give rise, by nature, are *moral* in character and that (b) the only objective motivating reasons to which prudential prescriptions give rise, by nature, are *prudential* in character. Accordingly, if the Exclusionary Thesis and the Sanctions Thesis are both true, then any telling that counts as authoritative gives rise to both an objective first-order *prudential* motivating reason *and* an objective second-order exclusionary *prudential* motivating reason. Only the Sanctions Thesis can explain the conceptual normativity of authoritative guidance, as that notion was explained in Section 8.

15 Objections: Of Angels and Emergency Volunteers

There are two objections that should be addressed here. One of them, Joseph Raz's society-of-angels argument, is directed at the claim that it is a necessary condition for a normative system to count as one of *law* that some of its mandatory norms are backed by a sanction. But it is worth considering what, if anything, the society-of-angels argument might tell us about the nature of *authority*. The second owes to David Estlund.[119] Though it is concerned with *morally legitimate* authority, it can teach us something interesting about the nature of practical authority.[120]

According to Raz's society-of-angels argument, there can exist among morally perfect beings a normative system lacking sanctions that counts as

---

[119] Estlund, *Democratic Authority*.

[120] Hart rejects that legal systems are inherently coercive on the ground it would constitute them as "gunmen writ large," but this is just silly. First, every legal system that has existed has backed laws prohibiting violence with a sanction. However, no one apart from a philosophical anarchist would claim this constitutes a legal system as analogous to a gunman. Second, I have been threatened with a loaded gun in my life and I am sure that no one who has ever had that harrowing experience would be remotely tempted to think law constitutes a gunman writ large just because it punishes violence. Most of us have disobeyed a traffic law at some point in our lives; though that might not be legally or morally justified, it is not irrational. In contrast, it is obviously irrational, absent unusual circumstances, to refuse to surrender the contents of one's wallet to a robber.

　　The gunman writ large argument is much weaker for other species of authoritative guidance because the associated liabilities are not as severe as those of the criminal justice system. Indeed, the only reason that there is a general *moral* problem of justifying practical authority is that authoritative tellings are backed, by nature, with a threat of detriment; absent this threat, there is nothing in our nonconceptual practices pertaining to authority that is plausibly presumed in need of moral justification.

one of law.[121] The worry is that such a system would include only norms that address pure coordination problems, like on which side of the road one ought to drive.[122] The system would not include any criminal norms prohibiting murder, assault, theft, or fraud because morally perfect subjects have no need, epistemic or practical, for such norms. Further, such a system would not include any norms pertaining to contracts or negligence because morally perfect subjects likewise have no need for these norms; an angel would never breach a contract unless released from it by the other parties and would always take the appropriate precautions to protect others from foreseeable injury.

What is left is an exceptionally thin system of norms that is not remotely equipped to do any of the jobs that have been done by every legal system in history. Notice that such a system would not include the so-called minimum content of natural law – which includes prohibitions of actions likely to lead to violent conflicts. Every system that constitutes one of law that has ever existed in our world has included, and enforced, the prohibitions of the minimum content of natural law. This is because we converge in believing, and justifiably so, that self-interested beings like us need to have these prohibitions backed by sanctions in order to enable us to live together in worlds of challenging material scarcity like ours. It is the content of law that helps to differentiates law from every other species of behavioral guidance, including those that define and govern the games we play.

It is worth noting that the society-of-angels argument cannot be extended to cover authoritative tellings in general.[123] Other species of authoritative guidance, like those of an employer or school, are less concerned with preventing harm than with ensuring subjects know how to do what they are required to do and can do such things competently. It is true that even employers and teachers need to back their tellings with sanctions, human nature being what it is, in order to deter enough harmful behavior to minimally achieve their ends. But practical authority's function in these cases is to ensure subjects can do what they need – or are needed – to do out in the world by guiding their behavior.

---

[121] Raz, *Practical Reason and Norms*, 159–160.

[122] A problem counts as one of pure coordination, as I intend the notion here, only if subjects have a stronger preference for agreement on a solution than for any particular solution to the problem. It is true some theorists have claimed the conceptual function of law is to coordinate behavior. But they are using the term *coordinate* in a much looser way than I am.

[123] It is worth noting that if the argument succeeds in refuting the applicability of the Sanctions Thesis to law, it also succeeds in refuting its applicability to authoritative guidance in general. The law, after all, is just one species of authoritative guidance. This is why it is helpful to consider whether the society-of-angels argument succeeds against its applicability to law.

This limits the reach of Raz's society-of-angels argument in the following way. The character of subjects matters with respect to evaluating conceptual theories of *law* because the most basic function of a legal system is to keep the peace among rational self-interested beings like us in worlds of acute material scarcity like ours. Law cannot do any of the other things we use law to do unless it is efficacious in preventing the war of all against all that constitutes the Hobbesian state of nature. But since the angels are morally perfect, there is no need for either criminal prohibitions or the sanctions backing them because there is no need to deter morally perfect beings from committing harmful acts.[124] In contrast, we are so far from being morally perfect – and, for that matter, from being even morally perfect*ible* – that it is just foolish to think we can learn anything about an institution contrived to enable *beings like us* to live in peace and reap the benefits of cooperation from beings with psychological features that inherently self-interested beings like us could never possess.[125]

Estlund's argument is not directly on point but is nonetheless quite helpful here. He points out that one can be *morally* bound to comply with a telling even when it is not backed with a sanction. That, of course, is obviously true, but it tells us nothing about the nature of practical authority. One might, for instance, be morally bound to comply with the tellings of a Samaritan who takes the initiative at the site of a bad automobile accident to direct traffic around the disabled cars. However, one can be morally obligated to do what another person says to do for reasons having nothing to do with authority – including that compliance is likely to conduce to the well-being of other people.

As it happens, the example is readily adapted to *support* the Sanctions Thesis. If a police officer with legal authority over the stretch of highway where the accident occurred *deputizes* the Samaritan, thereby authorizing her to *issue tickets with enforceable fines* to noncomplying drivers, then the Samaritan has something that counts as derivative authority over that stretch of highway for as long as she remains duly deputized. Such authorization is necessary to count as having practical authority over another person – as this Element has argued. While Estlund's observations may seem to problematize the analysis here, it turns out they actually support the Sanctions Thesis.

---

[124] Indeed, it is not metaphysically possible to deter a morally perfect being from committing an immoral act. Someone can be deterred from committing only those acts she is contemplating committing, and a morally perfect being is precluded, by her nature, from contemplating the commission of immoral acts.

[125] Mainstream philosophical and religious traditions in the West generally take the position that human nature is not perfectible and that human redemption requires faith in the grace of God. See, e.g., Harold Coward, *The Perfectibility of Human Nature in Eastern and Western Thought* (SUNY Press, 2012).

Conclusions

This Element attempts to provide a comprehensive theory of the nature of practical authority. To that end, it argues for two principal theses. The first is that the following claim exhausts the constitutive properties of authoritative tellings: authoritative tellings (1) tell subjects what to do; (2) create reasons to comply; (3) are issued by personal beings and govern the behavior of personal beings; (4) are issued by rationally competent beings and govern the behavior of rationally competent beings; (5) are issued under a claim of right that counts as plausible in virtue of being grounded in a system that subjects accept or acquiesce to as governing their behavior; (6) are issued by beings with the power to impose their will on subjects with respect to what they do; and (7) create obligations to comply.

The second thesis is that the claim that only tellings that are backed by the threat of a sanction count as authoritative (the Sanctions Thesis) can be inferred from each of the claims of the list, either as a logical implication or as the best explanation of why that claim is true – apart from claim (3) that authoritative tellings are issued only by personal beings and govern the behavior of only personal beings. Accordingly, this Element argues that all but one of these constitutive properties are uniquely explained by the Sanctions Thesis.

Bibliography

Robert Alexy, "Law and Correctness," *Current Legal Problems*, vol. 51, no. 1 (1998), 205–221

Maria Alvarez and Jonathan Way, "Reasons for Action: Justification, Motivation, and Explanation," in Edward N. Zalta and Uri Nodelman (eds.), *The Stanford Encyclopedia of Philosophy* (Fall 2024 edition), https://plato.stanford.edu/archives/fall2024/entries/reasons-just-vs-expl/

Harry Beran, *The Consent Theory of Political Obligation* (Croon Helm, 1987)

Stefan Bertea, *A Theory of Legal Obligation* (Cambridge University Press, 2019)

Allen Buchanan, *Justice, Legitimacy and Self-Determination* (Oxford University Press, 2004)

Harold Coward, *The Perfectibility of Human Nature in Eastern and Western Thought* (SUNY Press, 2012)

Roger Crisp, "Prudential and Moral Reasons," in Daniel Star (ed.), *The Oxford Handbook of Reasons and Normativity* (Oxford University Press, 2018), pp. 800–820

David Enoch, "Reason-Giving and the Law," in Leslie Green and Brian Leiter (eds.), *Oxford Studies in Philosophy of Law: Volume 1* (Oxford University Press, 2011), pp. 1–38

David Estlund, *Democratic Authority* (Cambridge University Press, 2007)

Leslie Green, *The Authority of the State* (Oxford University Press, 1989)

H. L. A. Hart, *The Concept of Law*, 3rd ed. (Clarendon Press, 2012)

Kenneth Einar Himma, *Coercion and the Nature of Law* (Oxford University Press, 2020)

    Morality and the Nature of Law (Oxford University Press, 2019)

    "The Practical Otiosity of Exclusionary Reasons," *Canadian Journal of Jurisprudence* (forthcoming 2024)

Frank Jackson, *From Metaphysics to Ethics: A Defense of Conceptual Analysis* (Oxford University Press, 2000)

Daniel Kahneman, *Thinking Fast and Slow* (Farrar, Straus and Giroux, 2011)

Daniel Kahneman and Amos Tversky, "The Framing of Decisions and the Psychology of Choice," *Science*, vol. 211, no. 4481 (1981), 453–458

Hugo Lagercrantz, "The Emergence of Consciousness: Science and Ethics," *Seminars in Fetal and Natal Development*, vol. 17, no. 5 (2014), 300–305

John Locke, *Second Treatise on Civil Government*, ed. C. B MacPherson (Hackett, 1990)

David McNaughton and Piers Rawling, "Motivating Reasons and Normative Reasons," in Daniel Star (ed.), *The Oxford Handbook of Reasons and Normativity* (Oxford University Press, 2018), pp. 171–196

Robert Nozick, *Anarchy, State, and Utopia* (Basic Books, 1977)

   The Nature of Rationality (Princeton University Press, 1993)

Plato, *Euthyphro, Apology and Crito*, trans. F. J. Church (Macmillan, 1948)

John Rawls, *Political Liberalism* (Columbia University Press, 1996)

Joseph Raz, "About Morality and the Nature of Law," *American Journal of Jurisprudence*, vol. 48, no. 1 (2003), 1–15

   Ethics in the Public Domain (Clarendon Press, 1994)

   Practical Reason and Norms (Oxford University Press, 1999)

Martha Stout, *The Sociopath Next Door* (Harmony Books, 2005)

Judith Jarvis Thomson, *The Realm of Rights* (Harvard University Press, 1990)

Daniel Wodak, "What Does 'Legal Obligation' Mean?" *Pacific Philosophical Quarterly*, vol. 99, no. 4 (2018), 790–816

Robert Paul Wolff, *In Defense of Anarchism* (Harper & Row, 1970)

Cambridge Elements ≡

Philosophy of Law

Series Editors

George Pavlakos
University of Glasgow

George Pavlakos is Professor of Law and Philosophy at the School of Law, University of Glasgow. He has held visiting posts at the universities of Kiel and Luzern, the European University Institute, the UCLA Law School, the Cornell Law School and the Beihang Law School in Beijing. He is the author of *Our Knowledge of the Law* (2007) and more recently has co-edited *Agency, Negligence and Responsibility* (2021) and *Reasons and Intentions in Law and Practical Agency* (2015).

Gerald J. Postema
University of North Carolina at Chapel Hill

Gerald J. Postema is Professor Emeritus of Philosophy at the University of North Carolina at Chapel Hill. Among his publications count *Utility, Publicity, and Law: Bentham's Moral and Legal Philosophy* (2019); *On the Law of Nature, Reason, and the Common Law: Selected Jurisprudential Writings of Sir Matthew Hale* (2017); *Legal Philosophy in the Twentieth Century: The Common Law World* (2011), *Bentham and the Common Law Tradition*, 2nd edition (2019).

Kenneth M. Ehrenberg
University of Surrey

Kenneth M. Ehrenberg is Professor of Jurisprudence and Philosophy at the University of Surrey School of Law and Co-Director of the Surrey Centre for Law and Philosophy. He is the author of *The Functions of Law* (2016) and numerous articles on the nature of law, jurisprudential methodology, the relation of law to morality, practical authority, and the epistemology of evidence law.

Associate Editor

Sally Zhu
University of Sheffield

Sally Zhu is a Lecturer in Property Law at University of Sheffield. Her research is on property and private law aspects of platform and digital economies.

About the Series

This series provides an accessible overview of the philosophy of law, drawing on its varied intellectual traditions in order to showcase the interdisciplinary dimensions of jurisprudential enquiry, review the state of the art in the field, and suggest fresh research agendas for the future. Focussing on issues rather than traditions or authors, each contribution seeks to deepen our understanding of the foundations of the law, ultimately with a view to offering practical insights into some of the major challenges of our age.

Cambridge Elements ≡

Philosophy of Law

Printed in the United States
by Baker & Taylor Publisher Services